CW00957398

Rosa Luxemburg:
An Intimate Portrait

ROSA LUXEMBURG: AN INTIMATE PORTRAIT

MATHILDE JACOB

TRANSLATED BY HANS FERNBACH WITH AN INTRODUCTION BY DAVID FERNBACH

Lawrence & Wishart
LONDON
in association with Heretic Books

Lawrence & Wishart Limited
99a Wallis Rd
London E9 5LN

First published 2000

English translation and Introduction
copyright © 2000 Heretic Books

All rights reserved. Apart from fair dealing for the purpose
of private study, research, criticism or review, no part of
this publication may be reproduced, stored in a retrieval
system, or transmitted, in any form or by any means,
electronic, electrical, chemical, mechanical, optical,
photocopying, recording or otherwise, without the prior
permission of the copyright owner.

British Library Cataloguing in Publication data
A catalogue record for this book is available
from the British Library.

ISBN 0 85315 900 9

Front cover: Self-portrait by Rosa Luxemburg. c.1911

Contents

Rosa Luxemburg in her study, c. 1910

Acknowledgement

The first authentic publication of Mathilde Jacob's memoir, "Von Rosa Luxemburg und ihren Freunden in Krieg und Revolution 1914–1919", was in the journal *Internationale wissenschaftliche Korrespondenz zur Geschichte der deutschen Arbeiterbewegung* [International Scientific Correspondence on the History of the German Workers' Movement], 24:4 (1988). Editors Rüdiger Zimmermann and Sybille Quack collated the two main versions of the text, and supplied copious annotation. Their permission for the present translation to be based on their edition is gratefully acknowledged, likewise that of Susanne Jacob as heir to the original copyright.

Introduction

Eighty years after her death, Rosa Luxemburg remains one of the most fascinating political figures of twentieth-century Europe. She did not lead a successful revolution, as she certainly wished to do, nor run a state, as she might have had to do. Yet she stands out as a brave and inspirational character, and a woman of outstanding integrity and compassion. Paradoxically, it was the very failure of her project that defined her place in history. Rosa Luxemburg was above all a Marxist, at a time when socialism could still credibly believe itself a 'science', both predicting and promoting the liberation of the working class by its own revolutionary action. Only with the First World War did this doctrine begin to break down, when the socialist parties of the leading industrial countries lined up behind their warring governments, and Lenin managed to seize power in backward Russia. The conflict between reformists and revolutionary adventurists in defeated Germany was the context of Rosa Luxemburg's brutal murder in January 1919. Yet while her classical Marxism of majority revolution found little practical application in subsequent decades, Rosa Luxemburg's writings, and the mind and personality these expressed, represented for much of the twentieth century the aspiration of a return to a socialism both radical and democratic, against the timidity of mere reformism and the authoritarian rigidity of Bolshevism. Though Marxist socialism may no longer be adequate to the problems of today, it remains a necessary and noble stage in the long haul of human emancipation, and Rosa Luxemburg the last of its classical exponents.

Rosa Luxemburg's family were Jewish, her native language Polish; born in 1871, she grew up within the Russian empire before escaping to the freedom of Switzerland. But it was eventually in Germany, the undisputed centre of international socialism at the time, that she made her home; within months of her move to Berlin in 1898, her intellectual gifts and her political passion had won her a place as a leading — if controversial — light in the Social-Democratic Party (SPD), a position she maintained for sixteen years, until the outbreak of the Great War. At the turn of the century she was the leading opponent of the 'revisionist' Eduard Bernstein, aligned with the party's 'Marxist centre' in maintaining its revolutionary tradition. After the Russian revolution of 1905, during which she returned to Poland, was arrested, and narrowly escaped a long prison term, Rosa Luxemburg sought to introduce into German socialism the extra-parliamentary tactics of the mass strike that had marked the Russian uprising. This brought a parting of the ways with Karl Kautsky and August Bebel, the SPD's intellectual and practical leaders, and by the time that world war threatened, the radical left was small and isolated.

In Germany, as in Britain and France, it is sobering to realise how few were the voices that held to their internationalist convictions when the time came to turn words into deeds. Even on the left of the SPD there were many who suddenly discovered Germany's mission to defend Europe against Russia. When on 4 August the German Socialists voted in the Reichstag to approve war credits, Rosa Luxemburg felt terrifyingly isolated. But from the very first, her stand against the war was absolute and unwavering. She was the anchor to which those socialists who remained true to their principles rallied, their forces steadily growing — if far too slowly — until after four long and dreadful years the mass of German workers did respond to her call, at least sufficiently to precipitate an end to a war that was already lost, and to overthrow the Kaiser.

Until communications were broken by the war, Rosa Luxemburg had kept close links with the socialist movement in her native Poland, which was no small component of that in the tsarist empire as a whole. In this context she had always opposed Lenin's concept of the party as an élite body of 'professional revolutionaries', predicting as early as 1904 that this would lead to a new dictatorship. If revolution was to be the action of the working class itself, then revolutionaries should stay with the mass party of that class. Even when the SPD supported the war, and the 'political truce' at home, Rosa Luxemburg and her friends sought to stay within the workers' party while organising their own propaganda and agitation. When the SPD expelled the anti-war opposition in 1917, she continued the same tactic within the USPD, the 'Independent' party formed by the expellees. The group which first of all called itself the 'Internationale group' after a journal that was closed down by the government on its first issue, and became known as the 'Spartacus group' after the pseudonym used by Rosa Luxemburg on an illegal leaflet, had no formal membership until the revolution of November 1918. Those prepared for clandestine activity formed a loose network based on mutual trust. This suited the work of a group formed for propaganda and agitation; it would not have suited the seizure of power in a revolutionary situation, but that was not Rosa Luxemburg's aim.

Revolution is almost by definition a time of confusion, in which radically new ideas are required. When the imperial regime was overthrown in November 1918 — the only successful popular uprising in German history — a situation arose in which, as Rosa Luxemburg realised, there were no easy answers. Workers' and soldiers' councils formed in each city as the regime crumbled, and their national body claimed political power in the name of the working class. At the same time, the last imperial Chancellor, Prince Max von Baden, handed over his office — smoothly, if not constitutionally — to the Social-Democrat leader Friedrich Ebert. The workers' councils endorsed a government under Ebert of the two socialist parties, with the SPD and the USPD each having three members; but the councils proved ineffective at exercising any control over the government, and prepared to give way to a Constituent Assembly to be elected in January. Ebert, meanwhile, bent his efforts to suppressing the revolutionary movement in alliance with the imperial general staff.

A further factor shaping events in Germany was the Bolshevik revolution in Russia, where Lenin had now been in power for a year. Rosa Luxemburg in her prison cell had written a critical analysis of Soviet policy, and saw the suppression of opposing parties as an ominous sign. Yet to the revolutionary movement in Germany, and to most of the Spartacus activists, Lenin's success was an example to follow. When at the Spartacus congress on 29–31 December, Rosa Luxemburg reluctantly agreed to break with the Independents and form the group into a new Communist Party of Germany, this was in large part a recognition of the inevitable. In the programme she wrote for the new party, however, she insisted that 'the Spartacus League will never take over government power except through the clear and unambiguous will of the great majority of the proletarian masses in the whole of Germany, never except by virtue of their conscious acceptance of the perspectives, goals and methods of struggle of the Spartacus League.'[1] This can be read as an explicit rejection of the putschist tactics adopted by the Bolsheviks. She concluded her speech at the congress with the suggestion that the conquest of proletarian power might well be a work of decades.[2] Yet in the Berlin streets the revolutionary workers were fighting to maintain the positions they had won, against the military threat of right-wing repression, and against the political threat that the Constituent Assembly might yield an anti-socialist majority.

The crisis came to a head just one week later. The USPD ministers had resigned from Ebert's government in protest at its repression of the revolutionary movement, and Ebert moved to dismiss the Berlin police president Emil Eichhorn, an Independent supporter whom the revolutionaries saw as a bastion against counter-revolution. A joint action commitee was formed, with the Communists represented by Karl Liebknecht, the Independents under Georg Ledebour, and the revolutionary shop stewards. Newspaper buildings were occupied, including the *Vorwärts* of the SPD. For one mad moment the committee proclaimed itself a revolutionary government. ('But Karl,' Rosa Luxemburg allegedly said, 'what about our programme?') After a few days the revolutionaries were already seeking to surrender; but as a show of strength Ebert brought in the remaining loyal units of the imperial army which suppressed the movement with heavy casualties. Berlin was gripped by a white terror, and after a week in hiding, Rosa Luxemburg and Karl Liebknecht were arrested and brutally murdered.

To the bourgeoisie, Rosa Luxemburg was especially a figure of hate — a Jewish foreigner from Poland who threatened the sanctity of their property, portrayed in caricature and spiteful gossip as a crazy monster, inhuman and unwomanly. After her death it was important for her friends, both Communist and Social-Democrat, to counter this with the real Rosa Luxemburg they remembered, especially evident in the copious letters she wrote during her long years in prison, of which several editions were published in the 1920s.[3] A generation later, Rosa Luxemburg's letters became part of the literary heritage in both West and East Germany, and successive biographies, including that by Elzbieta Ettinger in English, disclose a personality that continues to hold a fascination transcending that of her politics. Rosa Luxemburg was a loyal and supportive friend, a lover of music, literature and art, a competent amateur painter and botanist, full of sympathy and compassion for the animal world as well as for human suffering. Though socialist politics was for her both a duty and a passion, it was not the centre of her life as a human being. As she wrote to Luise Kautsky: 'I must have *someone* who believes me that it's only by mistake that I circle round the maelstrom of world history, and am really born to tend geese.'[4] Mathilde Jacob records a similar sentiment on p.97 below.

In this respect Rosa Luxemburg could not be further from Lenin, her opposite in both political and personal terms. A compelling question today, however, is what connection obtains between the personal and the political. Was Rosa Luxemburg a political figure who happened to be a most sympathetic human being, or did her distinctive human qualities inspire her politics in a significant way? The more Rosa Luxemburg's life is studied, the more clearly the latter alternative seems inescapable, and this despite her own protestations. She resisted, for example, the notion that being a woman should give her any particular perspective on society; she and her friend Clara Zetkin liked to describe themselves in jest as 'the last two men in the Social-Democratic Party', referring to their uncompromising radicalism. Yet the depth of both women's reaction to the senseless world war suggests an empathy with suffering more readily felt from the feminine side, and certainly contrasts markedly with the response of Lenin, who saw the war as an opportunity for revolutionary advance.

But the personal roots of Rosa Luxemburg's politics are more specific than feminine empathy, or a disinclination for the masculine games of power politics. No one can read her letters without being struck by her concern for individual human beings, whether close to her or more remote. And what should one make of such remarks as this:

> Everything would be much easier to cope with, moreover, if I would not forget the basic commandment I have made myself for life: the main thing is to be *good*! Simply and solely to be *good*, that resolves and ties up everything, and is better than all cleverness and knowall-ism.[5]

Not even to *do* good, and an injunction more in the spirit of the Christian gospel than a Kantian categorical imperative. Rosa Luxemburg's preference for informal organisation, and her motto that 'freedom is freedom for those who think differently', indeed have a deep psychological foundation.

As interest in the personal dimension of Rosa Luxemburg's life has increased in recent decades, so this memoir by Mathilde Jacob has become an indispensable and important source on the dramatic years of war and revolution. It was unknown to Rosa Luxemburg's first biographer, Paul Frölich, in the 1930s; Peter Nettl, in the 1960s, did not bother to consult it. More recently, however, Elzbieta Ettinger in the 1980s made considerable use of it, and still more so Annelies Laschitza in the most recent major biography.[6] Mathilde Jacob has been the subject of scholarly articles in Germany, and even a book that subtitles her as 'Rosa Luxemburg's best woman friend'.[7] Such

comparisons are odious. Rosa Luxemburg would not have classi-
fied her friends in rank order, and Mathilde Jacob would not have
claimed such a position. Clara Zetkin and Luise Kautsky, for example,
had both been friends of Rosa Luxemburg since 1898, and had a
common history that Mathilde Jacob did not share. Clara Zetkin
was certainly closest to Rosa Luxemburg as a political friend, and
Luise Kautsky was perhaps a unique confidante of Rosa Luxemburg's
emotional life. In subsequent Communist historiography (which
had reason for bias against her), Mathilde Jacob was referred to as
Rosa Luxemburg's 'secretary', and, as she explains, it was through
this kind of assistance that their connection began. Until the end,
Mathilde looked to Rosa as a superior being, and was quite content for their relationship to have a certain inevitable onesidedness.
But Mathilde soon became for Rosa an intimate friend, an indispensable support in her prison confinement, her main channel of
communication with the outside world, and the recipient of some
hundred and fifty letters.

Mathilde's carefully chosen title for her text was 'On Rosa
Luxemburg and Her Friends in War and Revolution 1914–1919'.
The 'friends' who appear in these pages are the select band of leading
figures in the Spartacus group who were both personal and politi-
cal friends of Rosa Luxemburg: Leo Jogiches, Karl Liebknecht, Franz
Mehring, Clara Zetkin and Paul Levi. In each case their role in
Mathilde Jacob's narrative needs a brief supplement here.

Leo Jogiches (1867–1919), from Vilna in Lithuania, was also
an émigré in Switzerland where he met Rosa Luxemburg in 1891,
and in 1894 they founded together the Social-Democratic Party of
the Kingdom of Poland (SDiKP).[8] For fifteen years Leo and Rosa
were lovers, and with some reluctance he followed her to Berlin
in 1900. As their correspondence shows (only Rosa's side survives),[9]
the partnership was stormy; Rosa aspired to a conventional mari-
tal situation, but Leo would not accept their relationship being
public knowledge, and would not let Rosa have a child. Rosa finally broke off the relationship in 1906, and took as a lover Costia
Zetkin, the 21-year-old son of her friend Clara. When Leo returned
to Berlin the following year, after escaping from tsarist prison, he
was incensed and periodically violent, yet he insisted on keeping
his room in Rosa Luxemburg's flat and spying on her personal life.
For the next few years Rosa maintained a brusque coldness towards
him, though she continued to collaborate with him in leading the
illegal Polish party. Leo had never involved himself in German
affairs, and not having the German nationality which Rosa Luxemburg
had acquired through a marriage of convenience, this would not

have been possible for him legally. By the time Mathilde met Leo
Jogiches, in January 1915, a new phase had evidently begun in his
relationship with Rosa, a platonic friendship in which he was at
last prepared to support her without seeking to control.

As Mathilde explains, during Rosa's imprisonment Leo suc-
cessfully ran the Spartacus Group's illegal activities until his own
arrest in March 1918. He always remained Rosa's closest political
confidant, even when as in December 1918 she did not follow his
advice against founding a Communist Party. Mathilde evidently
developed a great admiration for this master of conspiracy, whom
she worked with closely until he too was murdered only weeks
after Rosa Luxemburg. Her memoir is one of the few biographical
sources on Leo Jogiches, who remains little known even today.

Karl Liebknecht (1871–1919) is the name most commonly coupled
with Rosa Luxemburg, above all because of their martyrdom together. In the world of German Social-Democracy, Karl complemented
Rosa in many ways, and this was precisely his importance to her.
He was the son of a famous Social-Democrat pioneer, Wilhelm
Liebknecht, and named after Wilhelm's friend and teacher Karl
Marx. He was a member of the Reichstag, a native German, not
even Jewish, and of course a man. Curiously in view of his post-
humous celebrity, Liebknecht was not a convinced Marxist, holding
to an eclectic subjective philosophy of his own. But for several years
before the war Liebknecht had specialised in anti-militarist activity,
and his denunciation of the war in the Reichstag in December 1914
gave a signal to which oppositional forces across the country could
rally. As Mathilde writes on p.39, she had known Karl Liebknecht
before she met Rosa Luxemburg, though she did not develop the
same personal closeness that she had with Leo Jogiches as well as
with Rosa herself. Indeed, even in his lifetime she made pertinent
criticisms of Liebknecht's political style (ibid), and after he and
Rosa were murdered, she expressed her hostility to him most forcefully
in a letter to Clara Zetkin (below, p.128).

Franz Mehring (1846–1919) was a historical scholar and literary critic, and a colleague of Rosa Luxemburg at the SPD party
school, where she taught from 1908 to 1914. He and Clara Zetkin
were the two senior figures in the SPD who rallied to the radical
anti-war cause, though their work for Spartacus was limited by
the fact that Clara lived far from Berlin and was in poor health,
while Mehring in Berlin was already old and frail. As Mathilde
explains, it was originally through Mehring (and Julian Marchlewski)
that she came to know Rosa Luxemburg, though Mehring's appearance in her memoir is limited, and Mathilde does not seem

to have been on particularly close terms with him.

Clara Zetkin (1857–1933) was a pioneer of German socialism, a protégé of Frederick Engels, who developed the theory and practice of the Social-Democrat women's movement (as opposed to 'bourgeois feminism') as editor of the weekly newspaper *Gleichheit* [Equality] from 1892 to 1917. She befriended Rosa soon after her arrival in Germany, and the pair were seen as twin pillars of the radical left. The Zetkin household outside Stuttgart was always a second home for Rosa, though she had to conceal from Clara her relationship with Costia, and Clara's personal prickliness caused occasional frictions. When Rosa was first imprisoned, and Clara came to Berlin to visit her friend, she evidently warmed to Mathilde right away, and their connection remained close until they parted company politically in 1921.

Paul Levi (1883–1930), as well as appearing in Mathilde's narrative, is cited in a couple of passages from his own memoirs, and at the end of her text Mathilde reproduces his memorial speech on Rosa Luxemburg. Rosa had met Paul in Frankfurt in 1913, and engaged him as a lawyer when she was charged there for an anti-militarist speech. What was unknown until the 1980s, when Rosa's letters to him were first published, is that Paul also became her third and final lover, for a year at most until the passion cooled. Levi remained however Rosa's closest political protégé, and took over the leadership of the orphaned Communist Party after Leo Jogiches was killed in March 1919. As Mathilde explains towards the end of her memoir, she was then working closely with Paul Levi, and continued to do so after he was expelled from the Communist Party in 1921.

As well as an intimate friend of Rosa herself, Mathilde Jacob was thus one of the group of friends, forged through politics but bound by strong personal ties, that was distinctive of the Rosa Luxemburg circle. She was no intellectual or political figure in her own right, but held a distinct and respected place in this circle on the basis of her personal qualities and her commitment to the Spartacus cause. Through this connection, moreover, Mathilde developed both personally and politically, from the typist of stencils as she introduces herself at the start of the memoir, to having major responsibility in the threatened Communist Party at the end, not to mention her final offices for the dead Rosa Luxemburg that her laconic description only renders the more poignant.

What do we know of Mathilde Jacob? There is no detailed record of her early life, but some salient facts stand out. Born on 8 March

1873, thus two years younger than Rosa Luxemburg, she was from an assimilated Jewish family in Berlin. She completed secondary school, a level rather superior to that available for English girls at the time, but which did not lead on to higher education. Her father, a meat trader, went bankrupt and died in middle age. In about 1908, Mathilde took a flat in a lower-middle class building in the Moabit district, 11 Altonaerstrasse, where she lived with her widowed mother and a younger sister. Why she did not marry we can only speculate, but after studying bookkeeping, and working as a public stenographer, she ran from home a typing bureau, generally with just one assistant, also doing translations from French. She had a younger brother Harry, who worked for the trade-union movement and brought Mathilde her first clients from this and the Social-Democrat milieu.

From 1914, Mathilde's life was clearly centred on Rosa Luxemburg, and much of this emerges from her memoir. Mathilde conceals, however, or does not think worth revealing, the stresses that her wartime activity placed on her. From letters between her and Clara Zetkin, these were of various kinds. One was harassment by the police, who searched her home on several occasions, launched an investigation, but eventually failed to find any grounds for prosecuting her. (Mathilde had Leo's good training to thank for this.) Mathilde also suffered with her health, and eventually had to have an operation, possibly gynaecological, though she did not let this interrupt her political work for more than the absolute minimum. Financial worries were a further problem. As she writes to Clara Zetkin, she had to give up most of her professional work to make time for her political commitments.[10] And unlike the unnamed opportunists that she scathingly mentions in her memoir (p.85), Mathilde was not prepared to compromise her independence by taking a position with the Soviet embassy in Berlin when it opened in April 1918.

In the last pages of the memoir Mathilde's own initiatives become the centre of her narrative, and the reader will want to know what happened next. Shortly after Rosa Luxemburg's funeral Mathilde was arrested, and remained in prison from June to September 1919 without any specific charges being brought against her.[11] On her release she went to stay with Clara Zetkin in Stuttgart, where she remained until the summer of 1920, helping Clara to establish the first Communist women's journal *Die Kommunistin.* By this time the political situation had settled down somewhat, Clara Zetkin and Paul Levi had been elected as the first Communists to the Reichstag, and Mathilde moved back to Berlin, working as per-

sonal assistant to Levi. In November 1920 Levi succeeded in con-
solidating and expanding the Communist Party by winning over
the majority of the now-large Independent Socialist Party, but by
the new year his conflict with the Communist International came
to a head, as agents from Moscow sought to impose their own disastrous line on the German party. Levi resigned as leader in February
1921, and was expelled from the party in April after criticising the
putschist 'March action'.[12]

Paul Levi's letters to Mathilde from Moscow in summer 1920
show that she was throughout this crisis his close confidante, bound
by their common love for Rosa Luxemburg and their determina-
tion to uphold her political legacy. While Levi led the Communist
Party, Clara Zetkin also supported him strongly, but she had developed strong personal ties with Soviet Russia, and when Levi
and his followers, including Mathilde, were expelled, Clara remained
in the Bolshevised Communist Party. Mathilde seems to have had
no regrets, and in the open letter printed as an appendix to this
book, she defended herself from unfounded charges that Clara now
made. She followed Levi back into the SPD, where he remained a
leader of its left wing until his death in 1930, and worked closely
with him throughout this time. Levi's weekly journal, *Sozialistische
Politik und Wirtschaft* [Socialist Politics and Economics], was in
fact issued with Mathilde Jacob's name and address as responsible publisher. In the early 1930s she worked for *Die Weltbühne*
[The World Stage], the independent anti-fascist magaine edited by
Carl von Ossietsky.

Just as her modest role as 'secretary' had given Mathilde a certain
protection from police investigations during the World War, so when
Hitler came to power she was apparently seen as too unimportant
to be arrested for her socialist activity. For the next few years she
could continue her typing and translation business, though passing the normal retirement age. She maintained at least some illegal
political contacts: an isolated reference mentions her as warning
friends in 1939 against an untrustworthy comrade.[13] The main source
on her last years are the increasingly desperate letters she wrote
to Paul Levi's sister Jenny Herz in the USA, relating the failure of
her successive attempts to emigrate.[14] Like all remaining Jews in
Germany, she was subject to increasing restriction and humilia-
tion, until in July 1942 she was deported to Theresienstadt.[15] She
succumbed there on 14 April 1943. For forty years after the war
her name was little known, but from the 1980s a new wave of schol-
arship began to reveal the unique part she played in the Spartacus
years. In January 1997 a memorial tablet was erected outside the

town hall for Berlin's Tiergarten district, close to where she lived for most of her life, and the square renamed Mathilde-Jacob-Platz.

★   ★   ★

Mathilde Jacob started writing these reminiscences of her martyred friend within a year of Rosa Luxemburg's death, while staying with Clara Zetkin in Stuttgart. The surviving drafts, however, date from some ten years later, and only in a final version from around 1932 does she refer to it as a 'book', by which time it was too late to be published in Germany. The reasons for the delay are clear from the text itself. Mathilde was not a trained intellectual, nor an intuitively gifted writer, as she was herself well aware. She expresses herself clearly and competently enough, but has little sense of how a publishable book needs to be structured. She felt compelled, however, to bear witness, to the best of her ability, to 'a love that goes beyond the grave, love for a person and for a cause'.[16]

In June 1939 Professor Ralph H. Lutz of the Hoover Institution (Stanford University, California) visited Germany with the aim of acquiring socialist and communist archival material. Mathilde let him have an early version of her memoir, 153 letters to her from Rosa Luxemburg, and other related papers. She deposited a later version of the memoir with the archive of her deceased friend and colleague Paul Levi; indeed she organised this collection, which Levi's family took with them to Switzerland and later New York.[17]

Two main versions of Mathilde Jacob's memoir survive, along with two others that are merely fragments. The earlier version is more spontaneous in style, but leaves several references and gaps to be filled in later. The second has been somewhat stylistically flattened, possibly after consultation with a literary 'expert'. Much of the anecdotal material has been removed; on the other hand this text is supplemented by a number of relevant documents. In preparing the memoir for German publication in 1988, Rüdiger Zimmermann and Sybille Quack used the later version as a basis, appending material from the earlier version wherever this contained additional information or a contrasting perspective. This has been followed for the present edition, with material from the earlier version marked by pointed brackets < >, and a few sentences deleted from the later version where these are closely duplicated. Mathilde Jacob's own notes have been printed as footnotes on the page, and all editorial notes placed at the end. Section heads have been inserted to break up the text.

Mathilde Jacob, c. 1930

suchen. Das gab eine kleine Abwechslung; auch die Befolgung der
ärztlichen Vorschriften nahm Zeit und Interesse in Anspruch. Der
Arzt war Rosa Luxemburg sympathisch, bei ihren Besuchen unterhielt
sie sich gern mit ihm. Blieb bis zur Abfahrt des Zuges Zeit übrig
- die Züge fuhren recht selten - so unternahm die Gefangene einen
Spaziergang oder sie machte kleine Einkäufe. Dann erwartete ihn
der begleitende Beamte vor dem Eingang der Geschäfte. Er war nach
Rosa Luxemburgs Aussage bescheiden und zurückhaltend; wenn auch
ermüdet, so kehrte sie doch meist angeregt nach Wronke zurück.

In dieser Zeit ihrer Krankheit war Rosa Luxemburg unbe-
rechenbar launisch. In ihrer Reizbarkeit fürchtete sie, ich könnte
die ihr so unangenehme Oberin um etwas bitten. Sowies Rosa Luxemburg mich bei einem unerwarteten Besuch ab in der Annahme, ich
hätte die Oberin um diesen Besuch gebeten. In Wirklichkeit hatte
mir der Staatsanwalt, selbst ängstlich wegen Rosa Luxemburgs Ge-
sundheitszustand, angeboten, des öfteren zu ihr zu gehen, damit sie
dadurch Freude und Ablenkung hätte.

Als sie sich nun weigerte, mich zu empfangen, suchte ich,
traurig darüber, meine Zuflucht im Walde. Ich machte mir klar,
wieviel Rücksicht wir Rosa Luxemburg schuldig waren. So mit Ge-
danken beschäftigt, sah ich an den Ufern eines Teiches durch das
Grün herzförmiger Blätter viele weisse Blüten leuchten. Es war
Sumpfkalla. Ich zog Schuh und Strümpfe aus und wagte vorsichtig
einige Schritte in den Morast, um die Blumen zu pflücken. Auf dem
Rückwege gab ich sie im Gefängnis ab.

Als die Pforte geöffnet wurde, winkte Rosa Luxemburg mit
dem Taschentuch aus ihrem Gärtchen. Ich eilte an das Gitter.

"Sind Sie bös?"

"Ach, wie könnte ich das!"

"Ich habe schon zu Frau Doktor gesagt", liess sich die
Stimme der Oberin vernehmen, "wenn ich Fräulein Jacob wäre, würde

A page from the typescript of Mathilde Jacob's memoir,
'Rosa Luxemburg and her Friends in War and Revolution 1914 – 1919'

1. The Birth of a Friendship

My personal connection with Rosa Luxemburg began when I was given work for the *Sozialdemokratische Korrespondenz*.* <Never before had a woman made such a deep impression on me. Her large, brilliant eyes which seemed to understand everything, her modesty and goodness, her childish joy at everything beautiful, made my heart beat faster for her. I gazed in admiration at this elevated spirit, who was almost shabbily dressed. Though I often subsequently accompanied her to meetings, conferences or demonstrations, the first impression remained: she looked so modest and unpretentious that people who had not seen her before cried out in amazement: 'That's Rosa Luxemburg?' When she then spoke in her emotional style, she grew beyond her tender little figure and fascinated her listeners.>

Rosa Luxemburg had founded this *Korrespondenz* jointly with Julian Karski** and Franz Mehring,*** with the aim of combatting the steadily spreading revisionism in the old Social-Democratic party. Karski and Mehring dictated their articles in my office. In order to save Rosa Luxemburg the journey and effort, her manuscripts were also dictated by these two. But this procedure meant that small mistakes sometimes occurred, and as Rosa Luxemburg hated printer's errors in her work she eventually came to me herself.

'You are a master on your machine,' she said after we had briefly worked together on her first visit. Contact was immediately established between us, and when she had finished her dictation she

---

* <This appeared from 27 December 1913 to 21 December 1914, duplicated from typewritten stencils.>
** The *nom de plume* of Dr Julian Marchlewski, born 17 May 1866, died 2 March 1925, one of Rosa Luxemburg's closest comrades-in-arms. Their friendship dated from the student days together in Switzerland.[1]
*** Dr Franz Mehring, born 22 February 1846, died 29 January 1919, historian and literary scholar, joined the Social-Democrat party after thorough study of Marxist doctrine, which he formerly had combatted from the bourgeois camp in word and writing.[2]

offered to help with the duplicating. I said it was certainly not difficult but it needed practice. She replied that she was nimble, and I could give her some work with all confidence. So I showed her how to make the necessary corrections on the stencil. But the corrections made by Rosa Luxemburg did not show up properly on duplication. 'Oh,' she said, 'I'm no use even for this!'

The articles in this *Korrespondenz*, designed for the Social-Democratic press, overshadowed the other Social-Democratic publications by the comprehensive knowledge and gripping style of their authors. The *Korrespondenz* was avidly read by editors, but only a few papers of Marxist tendency reprinted the articles. During the war the *Korrespondenz* like all publications of the radical left was subject to censorship, which stopped all criticism of the prevailing conditions. Further appearance was impossible and the fight had to be continued illegally.

Two groups within the SPD fought against the war: the Haase-Ledebour[3] tendency and the Luxemburg-Mehring tendency. These two groups in no way confronted each other as enemies, and though they marched separately they generally fought and struck together. They held joint discussions, and despite all political differences the personal relations of Rosa Luxemburg, Franz Mehring and their followers to these comrades-in-arms were of a friendly nature.

The group around Haase and Ledebour, whose deputies after [nearly] eighteen months of war voted against war credits in the Reichstag on 21 December 1915 and subsequently called themselves the Arbeitsgemeinschaft [Ad Hoc Working Group], formed the nucleus of the later 'Independent' party [USPD]. They were always hesitant in raising their voice and were ever ready for compromise, forming the so-called political 'marsh'. The second group, very much smaller but consistently revolutionary-Marxist, which later became the Spartacus League, followed the brilliant leadership of Rosa Luxemburg. Franz Mehring stood at her side as an equal comrade-in-arms. After the outbreak of war Karl Liebknecht[4] joined them, and together with Otto Rühle[5] he first rejected war credits in the Reichstag session of 2 December 1914. Courageously and without fear, he raised his voice against the world war from then on and gave the Reichstag a lot of work with his 'petty questions'. As these were the only possible way to openly address the masses he asked such questions over and over again on every occasion, for which the disastrous conduct of the war gave ample opportunity.

This initially very small group — Franz Mehring once said to me jokingly, 'Tell Rosa she mustn't upset me, as I'm her only supporter'

— grew quickly and gained influence. Brave fighters ready to sacrifice themselves joined together to protest against the war, both
in Berlin and across the country. Scholarly lectures were also used
in the service of this struggle. Thus Rosa Luxemburg arranged for
the SPD in the autumn of 1914 a course of public lectures on the
'rise and development of capitalism'.[6] She started with the development of towns, the growth of a money economy, the craft guilds,
the discovery of America and the horrors of colonialism this involved, then passed on to modern industry and the industrial proletariat created by it. Pointing out the crises which modern capitalism
evokes offered the lecturer an opportunity to explain how the attempts to overcome these crises all necessarily led to the world
war.

Even if some of the numerous listeners who came to the Bartsch
assembly rooms in Neukölln on these Sunday mornings did not
always agree with her conclusions, everybody followed the mas-
terly dialectical expositions with keen interest. In the last lecture,
when the course leader thanked her for the rich instruction, he
played on Goethe's words to say at the end of his speech: 'To walk
with you, Frau Doktor, brings both honour and profit'.[7] Yes, it was
always profitable to walk with Rosa Luxemburg. It was part of her
nature to make her rich knowledge accessible to others.

'You must visit me sometime,' she said to me during the Neukölln
lectures, 'first of all because of Mimi, second to see my paintings
and third to give me pleasure.' Mimi was Rosa Luxemburg's cat.
One morning, when Rosa Luxemburg had arrived early in the class-
room of the party school where she gave lectures on political economy
before the war, she found this helpless little creature hurt by a
charwoman's broom which had fallen on it. Rosa Luxemburg took
care of the little animal, adopted it and brought it up. Her famili-
arity with the kitten grew steadily; she eventually talked to it about
her joys and sorrows. Whatever time of day or night she returned
home the kitten would caress her, sniff her handbag or parcels which
Rosa Luxemburg had brought back, and always find a titbit for itself.
Obviously Rosa Luxemburg considered carefully where Mimi should
go during her impending imprisonment.[8] This was set for 31 March
1915, but on 18 February she was suddenly arrested. The following letter written shortly before her arrest witnesses to her worry
about Mimi:[9]

Sunday
Dear Fräulein Jacob,
Many thanks for the charming flowers, and my favourites at
that, the sweet anemones!
You really have given me much pleasure. But the
Norddeutsche Allgemeine is right: the German people are so
wasteful, as if the fatherland were not in danger and distress.
How can we 'hold out' if the nation does not get more frugal? [....]
The idea with Mimi shows me that good spirits, yes
especially these, don't manage to grasp the weakness and fragility
of earthly things. Mimi carried in a basket, taken for a day and
then brought back! As if it was question of an ordinary creature of
the species *felis domestica*! Well, you should know, good spirit,
that Mimi is a little mimosa, a hyper-nervous little princess in
cat's fur, and when I, her own mother, once wanted to carry her
out of the house against her will, she got cramp due to the
excitement and turned stiff in my arms so that she had to be
brought back into the apartment with distressed little eyes and
only recovered after some hours. Yes, yes, you have no idea what
my motherly heart has already experienced. So, let's leave Mimi
in the flat. I am already terrified if I think of the unavoidable
transport — before 31st March, when I have to take her to the
house in Grunewald [...]
But if you come alone I shall be very pleased. Tomorrow and
the day after I have to make two 'unpostponable' business visits...
then I expect you on Wednesday — if you want to waste your
time as well as filthy lucre in coming to see me.
In the meantime with kindest regards,
Yours R.L.

Rosa Luxemburg owned many valuable folders of art prints. She
particularly loved the English painter Turner. She could not get
enough of the soft colours of his landscapes. She herself drew and
painted with much joy and genuine talent. Some of her drawings
and painted portraits have been preserved, including a self-portrait.
I believe my visits often gave Rosa Luxemburg pleasure. If there
was anything to be done for her, my motto was 'enough is not enough',
but all the same she was always the giving party. A conversation
with her, a glance from her understanding eyes accompanied by a
warm handshake, allowed many to resume life's struggle with renewed
hopes.

*   *   *

Towards the end of the lectures in Neukölln, Rosa Luxemburg fell
ill. The long journey from Südende[10] to the east of Berlin she found

very strenuous. Just the same she did not interrupt the course. But after its completion she went on medical advice into the Schöneberg hospital. <I still see her bearing patiently her pain, which proved to be a severe stomach condition. She would pull me to the edge of her bed when I tried to kiss her small, white hands by way of greeting. She did not allow this under any circumstances, laughed about such nonsense and heartily pulled me towards her. But most of the time she was not disposed to such tendernesses.> Here I met Leo Jogiches,[11] whose friendship with Rosa Luxemburg went back twenty-five years. I am grateful that fate made me witness to this friendship, which began during their university studies together in Zurich.

Leo Jogiches had an acute mind, wide knowledge and an excellent memory. It was he who forged ahead and was often even the dominant partner. There were times when Rosa Luxemburg completely adapted to his idiosyncracies. But then her fiery spirit cleared a path and made its own way once more, and it was not rare for a heated dispute to arise between her and her friend. No one except a few intimates had any idea how devoted Rosa Luxemburg was to Leo Jogiches. These two had such complete control over themselves that they did not disclose their feelings in front of others, either by a glance or a smile. They looked after each other and their friendship grew ever clearer and firmer. But this friendship did not prevent Leo Jogiches from being inexorable towards Rosa Luxemburg if it was a question of carrying out a political task. On one occasion Rosa Luxemburg said to me: 'Leo does not admit any reason which might hinder someone from carrying out their duty. Once when I was a student I was to give a lecture but felt physically so unwell that I feared I could not speak. I suggested to him that he should entrust the lecture to someone else. "Don't worry, just give the lecture," he said, "you'll be able to last out to the end." And indeed,' Rosa Luxemburg continued, 'I only collapsed after I had finished my lecture.'

<Leo Jogiches on his part once wanted to demonstrate to me Rosa Luxemburg's kindness. 'I had only recently met her,' he said, 'and complained that I had no tea; even then this was one of the most essential things in my life. Rosa had just received tea from her family in Poland. She immediately handed me a packet and said, "Please, here is some tea for you." Naturally I didn't take it,' Leo Jogiches added. And this way of acting was characteristic of him. It was hardly ever possible to get him to accept anything.>

Rosa Luxemburg's high conception of love and friendship is evidenced from a passage referring to Frau von Stein in a letter written to me [from prison] some time later, which I append here in full:[12]

Friday 9.4.15

My dear Fräulein Jacob,
    I hope these lines reach you in time for a Sunday greeting, as
I intended. Many hearty thanks for your letters, which I read
often and which bring me much cheer. Today came the second
(from Jena, where I don't know your hotel) with the lovely
enclosures. Mimi's picture gave me tremendous pleasure, I always
have to laugh when I look at it: I have often experienced these
scenes of her savagery when someone attempts to make
'advances' to her, so that I almost hear her snarling when I look at
the picture. It has come out marvellously well; I also find the
young doctor who shows such interest in my Mimi immediately
very sympathetic.
    A very special thanks for the flowers. You just don't know
what a boost they give me. I am now able to botanise again which
is a passion for me and the best recreation after work. I don't
know if I have already shown you my botanical folders in which I
have entered about 250 plants since May 1913, all splendidly
preserved. I have them all here as well as my various atlases, and
now I can start a new folder especially for the 'Barnimstrasse'.
But all those little flowers which you sent me I didn't yet have
and now I have placed them in my folder; I am particularly
pleased with the goldstar (the little yellow flower in the first
letter) and the pulsatilla, as these cannot be found here in Berlin.
Also the two ivy leaves from Frau von Stein are immortalised — I
did not have ivy (*Hedera helix* in Latin) in it properly; I am
doubly pleased about their origin. Apart from the liverwort, all
plants were very tidily pressed, which is important for botanising.
    I am glad for you that you are seeing so much; for me it
would be a punishment if I had to visit museums and the like. I
immediately get migraine and feel racked. The only relaxation for
me is to stroll about or lie in the grass in the sun where I observe
the tiniest bugs or stare up at the clouds. This *ad notam* for our
future journey together. I would not in the least prevent you from
visiting everything of interest to you but as far as I am concerned
you must excuse me. But you combine both, which is the best
way.
    I saw a portait of Lady Hamilton in the French XVIIIth
century exhibition. I cannot recall the name of the painter, just
remember a bold and loud structure, a robust and challenging
beauty which left me cold. My taste is for somewhat more refined
feminine types. I still see vividly in the same exhibition the
portrait of Madame de Lavalière by Lebrun, in silver-grey tone
which marvellously suited the translucent face, the blue eyes and
the light dress. I could hardly drag myself away from the picture
in which was embodied the whole refinement of pre-
revolutionary France, a genuine aristocratic culture with a light

suspicion of decay.

It is good that you are reading Engels's *Peasant War*. Have
you already finished the book by Zimmermann? Engels really
does not deal with the Peasant War historically but offers a
critical philosophy of it, the nourishing flesh of the facts is given
by Zimmermann. When I travel through the sleepy Wurtemberg
villages, between the fragrant dungheaps, and the hissing geese
with their long necks reluctantly make way for the car whilst the
hopeful village youth call out insults, I can never imagine that in
the same villages world history passed with thundering steps and
dramatic figures hustled about.

I am reading for relaxation the geological history of
Germany. Imagine, in Sweden clay slates have been found from
the Algonquin era, i.e. from the oldest period of the earth's
history before there was any trace of organic life, countless
millions of years ago — with imprints of raindrops from a brief
shower! I cannot tell you what a magic effect this distant greeting
from primeval times has on me. Nothing I read gives me such a
thrill as geology.

As regards Frau von Stein, with all respect for your ivy
leaves: God punish me, but she was a cow. When Goethe gave her
her marching orders she behaved like a screeching washerwoman,
and I stand on my opinion that the character of a woman does not
show itself where love starts but where it ends. Of all Goethe's
Dulcineas I like only the delicate, restrained Marianne von
Willemer, the 'Suleika' of the *Westöstliches Divan*. I am so glad
that you are recuperating. You need it. I am very well.

Hearty greetings,

Your R.L.

The treatment in the Schöneberg hospital had not yet been completed, but as soon as acute danger was no longer imminent Rosa
Luxemburg returned home again. <I accompanied the patient to
her home in Südende, where Leo Jogiches received us. Rosa Luxemburg with her weak physical strength fought tirelessly against the
rotten war policy. She experienced the collapse of the German Social-
Democratic Party in August 1914 with her heart saddened to death.
She felt herself personally humiliated by the defeat. To admit it
and to undertake new victorious campaigns was her first duty. To
be sure, the forces were lacking, yet Rosa Luxemburg had no doubt
about finding them.>

There were very few leading German party comrades with equally
acute perception at the outbreak of war. Rosa Luxemburg, Franz
Mehring and Clara Zetkin[13] had made an appeal to the workers of
the world which should have been signed also by those left-wing
Social-Democratic leaders who supported its contents: condem-
nation of the complete failure of the German Social-Democratic

Party, refusal of war credits, consolidation and firm integration of the Socialist International. Only one lone individual was prepared to sign the manifesto: Karl Liebknecht. <Rosa Luxemburg now had to work together with this lone individual in order to enlighten and shake up the masses by word and writing. Karl Liebknecht hurled his accusations loud and clear from the benches of the Reichstag into the world. It seemed a labour of Sisyphus, given the nationalistic frenzy that had gripped masses and leaders. It was not the worst comrades who at that time left the Social-Democratic party in disgust.

The German government knew only too well that Rosa Luxemburg, the fearless fighter, had to be excluded from political struggle so that the military camarilla could continue its criminal and mendacious policy. Talks given by Rosa Luxemburg in Neukölln, and some leaflets of which she was suspected of being the author, gave sufficient ground for her imprisonment. In none of her talks, indeed, had she missed the opportunity to relate the political-economic conditions of the past to the present, and show how unscrupulous the policy of the rulers had always been. On 18 February 1915 Rosa Luxemburg was arrested, no matter that she was still ill, to serve the one-year prison term she had been sentenced to by the Frankfurt criminal court.>[14]

Apart from this appeal Rosa Luxemburg had also written a second one directed against the party leadership and the Reichstag group. For this too she had asked the party oppposition for signatories. But all its supporters had qualms or hid behind excuses. Rosa Luxemburg continuously shortened the appeal. She was concerned to pin down those voices that stood up against the war policy. But no matter how she drafted it, nobody apart from Karl Liebknecht put his name next to the three upright spirits: Luxemburg, Mehring and Zetkin. To publish the protest against the party leadership and the Reichstag group proved an impossibility, the press refused to accept it.

The party leadership sent Richard Fischer to Switzerland to justify its stand to the International.[15] To counter this Rosa Luxemburg sent the protest against the party leadership and the Reichstag group to Switzerland to justify her opposite position. The call to the workers of the world was also smuggled abroad and made public there.[16] [When] Rosa Luxemburg was snatched from this activity and put into prison, Karl Liebknecht informed the Social-Democratic press by way of the following text, 'From the Obstructionists':[17]

On Thursday afternoon comrade Rosa Luxemburg was suddenly
arrested in her flat by two detectives. She was first taken by car to
the Berlin police headquarters, Dept VII (political police) and from
them in the green wagon[18] to the women's prison in Barnimstrasse.
Comrade Luxemburg was to serve the one-year prison sentence
imposed on her last year in Frankfurt-am-Main. By higher orders the
deferment of the sentence until 31 March was cancelled and the
immediate execution of the sentence ordered by telegraph. From a
paragraph in the *Deutsche Tageszeitung* which is amazingly rapidly
informed of the proceedings, probably on good authority, and which
honours our comrade by malicious comment, we learn that this
official interference is directly due to the political activity of
Comrade Luxemburg which is much disliked in certain quarters.
All signs point to the work of the dirty hands of police spies.

I managed to send Rosa Luxemburg a few lines in prison, and
received the calmly composed reply:[19]

Tuesday [23 February 1915]

My dear Fräulein Jacob!
Your letter on Sunday was the first written greeting which I
received from the outside world, and gave me much joy. Just now
I received the second, for which heartfelt thanks. Don't worry
about me; I am quite well both healthwise and 'mentally'. Nor
did the transport in the green wagon shock me: I already
experienced the same journey in Warsaw. No, it was so strikingly
similar that various pleasant thoughts occurred to me. Of course,
there was a difference: the Russian gendarmes escorted me as a
'political' with great respect, the Berlin police on the other hand
explained that they did not care who I was, and placed me with
nine 'colleagues' in a wagon. But all these are in the end trifles,
and never forget that whatever will come life is to be taken with
a calm mind and cheerfulness. These I possess here as well in the
necessary measure.
So that you do not get an exaggerated idea of my heroism I
shall admit remorsefully that when I had to undress to my
underwear for the second time that day, and submit to being
groped about, I could hardly restrain my tears. Obviously I was
furious with myself for such weakness, and still am... And what
upset me on the first evening was not so much the prison cell but
— guess! — the fact that I had to lie down without a nightdress
and without having combed my hair. Not to lack a classical
quotation here, do you remember the first scene in *Maria Stuart*
when her jewels were taken from her: 'To go without life's little
ornaments,' says Maria's lady-in-waiting, Lady Kennedy, 'is
harder than to bear great trials.'[20] (Schiller put it rather better
than I do here.) But what am I straying into? God punish England

and forgive me for comparing myself with an English queen! By
the way I have 'life's little ornaments' in the shape of
nightdresses, combs and soaps — they are all here thanks to the
angelic kindness and patience of Karl — and so life can run its
normal course. I am very glad that I get up so early (5.40) and only
wait for Madame Sun to kindly follow my example so that I can
get some benefit from my early rising. The best is that when
walking about in the courtyard I see and hear birds: a whole
swarm of cheeky sparrows who sometimes make so much noise
that I am surprised no tall policeman interferes. And then a few
blackbirds, the yellow-beaked male sings quite differently from
my blackbirds in Südende. He gabbles and screeches such
nonsense that I have to laugh. Perhaps in March or April he will
be ashamed and will warble properly. (Now I have to think of my
poor sparrows who will no longer find a table laid for them on my
balcony and will be sitting on the railing and wondering. Here
you must definitely shed a few tears, it is just too touching!)

Dear Fräulein Jacob, I bestow on you the highest honour I
can award a mortal being: I shall entrust you with my Mimi! But
you will have to await some definite news which you will get
from my lawyer. Then you'll have to abduct her in the car in your
arms (definitely not in a basket or sack!!!) with the help of my
housekeeper,[21] and it would be best if you take her along (I mean
just for the journey, not for life); she will pack all Mimi's seven
belongings (her little box, cat litter, bowl, cushions and — please!
— a red armchair which she is used to). All this, I suppose, can be
stowed in the car. But as I said, let us wait a few days.

And what are you doing now? Are you reading much? I hope
so. If it comes to it, I spend the whole day here reading, except
when I eat, go for a walk or clean the cell. The nicest is the close
of the day: the two quiet hours of daylight from 7 to 9 in the
evening when I can think and work.

Frau Zetkin was unfortunately so agitated that I am very
worried about her.

I give you my very hearty greetings, keep well and cheerful.
       Your R.L.

It goes without saying that I would be extremely pleased to
see you but unfortunately we will have to wait. I am only rarely
allowed visitors and for the time being my lawyers require access.
Please also collect your vase from my flat.

Clara Zetkin, who had been a friend of Rosa Luxemburg for many
years, had hurried from Stuttgart to Berlin on hearing of the arrest. She arranged the papers Rosa Luxemburg had left in her flat
and contrived permission to visit her pretending she was a sister-
in-law of the prisoner. Thus the worried Clara Zetkin was allowed
to talk to her. But this little ruse was soon discovered. One of the

warders recognised Clara Zetkin and informed the woman supervisor after the visit who the 'sister-in-law' really was. The supervisor, who already felt some sympathy for the new prisoner, was
generous enough to ignore this.

After a few days Clara Zetkin left, and apart from Leo Jogiches
there was nobody to look after Rosa Luxemburg. I asked to be allowed to help him. He declined and tried with the help of Rosa
Luxemburg's laundress to provide her with the essentials. This proved
to be too awkward, for the most part impossible, so that Leo Jogiches
asked for my help.

When she came out on a 'visit' Rosa Luxemburg herself gave
me full authority to take care of her flat and arrange all other matters
— naturally with help from Leo Jogiches. 'This was the lovely day
at home,' she noted on her calendar in the cell on 12th March,
and on the next page, 'this was the second lovely day.'[22] The court
had given her two days' leave from prison to enable her to settle
everything essential. I made some preparations to receive her in
the flat in Südende. When I heard a car I hurried into the street to
greet Rosa Luxemburg. "That is what I thought, that you would
be waiting for me," she said as she embraced me. Soon Leo Jogiches
and Karl Liebknecht joined us. Paul Levi,[23] Rosa Luxemburg's defence lawyer at the Frankfurt Criminal Court, who had become a
friend since this trial,[24] did not want to miss a favourable opportunity to see and talk to his client, and had come on an early train
from Frankfurt. Franz Mehring also came, and various other political friends shook Rosa Luxemburg's hand in the course of the
day.

When we sat down together episodes of prison experience were
exchanged. Karl Liebknecht told of his time in the fortress of Glatz
and of his father's imprisonments; Leo Jogiches of his and Rosa
Luxemburg's dungeons in Poland and Russia. Paul Levi could at
that time only mention a detention during his student days in Berlin,
whilst Franz Mehring was still quite unscathed.[25] They were two
happy days which left a bitter aftertaste when our friend said goodbye.
She comforted us, smiling. We waved from the balcony when the
car took her away. The accompanying prison wardress had been
forbidden to take any of us along in the car. Karl Liebknecht, with
his divine heedlessness of what was permitted or not, jumped into
the car as it moved off, and the guards, who had been charmed by
Liebknecht's kindness and courtesy during the two days, did not
object to his accompanying.

In prison Rosa Luxemburg was responsible for providing her
own food for which 60 Mark had to be paid monthly. The Social-

Democratic party executive took care of this, whilst a well-off party friend placed at our disposal the necessary extra for the rent of the flat and other expenses. At this time I was unaware that Rosa Luxemburg was quite without means, nor did I know about the necessary expenses. Leo Jogiches avoided telling me; he just went through with me from time to time the costs I had incurred. Neither did I know at that time how harmful the prison food was for the suffering Rosa Luxemburg. I was told that she received hospital food, which relieved me. Only later did I learn how bad this was, sometimes even inedible; for Rosa Luxemburg never complained or asked for anything. She was always cheerful, worked and refreshed herself with interesting books. After some seven months in prison Rosa Luxemburg's physical condition worsened so much that she had to stay part of the time in bed. Probably on the doctor's order the supervisor now allowed me to bring some extra food — 'once a week and not much,' she stipulated.

Once a month Rosa Luxemburg was allowed to have visitors. The first to seek out their friend were Dr Franz Mehring and his wife. Two or three other friends were allowed to come, but at Rosa Luxemburg's wish I was to take up the remaining visiting opportunities, as she thought the smuggling was best in my hands. Likewise the prisoner was only allowed to write and receive letters once a month, but the governor did not enforce this rule strictly, so that we could more often send a few lines. We even sent flowers which as a convicted prisoner she was really not supposed to have. When, at the beginning, I wanted to hand in the flowers, the official on duty looked into Rosa Luxemburg's file and said, 'As you insist, the flowers can remain here. But the prisoner has five convictions, we are not allowed to give them to her.' All the same she was given them, and she stuck a number of flowers she was given, this time and later, in her album labelled 'Barnimstrasse 10, Cell 219'.

*　　*　　*

Right at the start of her imprisonment Rosa Luxemburg set to work, to expose the treason to socialism committed by the party's leadership. The result was titled *The Crisis in German Social-Democracy* and has become known throughout the world as the Junius pamphlet.[26] <Karl Liebknecht frequently went to see Rosa Luxemburg, who unobtrusively gave him articles or pamphlets whilst with assumed innocence he handed her a newspaper containing prohibited articles or reports. He acted as Rosa Luxemburg's lawyer so that he could at any time obtain access to her, even though under supervision.>

After he made himself increasingly awkward, Liebknecht was sent to the front as a soldier, and thereafter Leo Jogiches had me take political reports to the prison; Rosa Luxemburg's comments on these, her articles, texts for leaflets and other material got out the same way. Rosa Luxemburg and I were indefatigable in devising new ways of smuggling, which often were very time-consuming. For written communications we agreed on a code word or a sign confirming the receipt.

It frequently happened that these confirmations took an unusually long time. We then suffered tortures of anxiety. We trembled for one another over the penal servitude which would have been the consequence if our secret correspondence had been discovered. If the confirmation was too long in coming then even Leo Jogiches grew restless and tried to comfort me. Rosa Luxemburg knew in an exemplary way how to give signs and hints in her censored letters, and to strengthen our courage. Thus on 3 Oct 1915 she wrote:[27]

> My dear Fräulein Jacob,
> You have suddenly made me so rich and cheerful that I have to thank you straight away. Really with you it's like in the fairy tale, 'Table, lay yourself.' The other day I'd hardly uttered the wish for a nice letter when it was already here. And just now I was sitting a little depressed when the glorious bouquet of flowers again brought so much colour and fragrance into the place, as well as the feeling that you were near. If I just could have seen you for a moment! First of all, the most important thing: the flowers. Do you know what treasures you have sent me? But anyway, the smaller yellow ones with the brown velvety centre are elecampane (*Inula helenium*), the large yellow ones which look like sunflowers are Jersualem artichoke (*Helianthus tuberosus*), finally the tiny yellow one with the many little clusters and a lovely smell is a Canadian golden rod (*Solidago virgaurea*), all three from the family of composites. The beautiful red-yellow coloured little leaves are naturally from a rowan, the blood-red branch is a prunus or 'turkish cherry', the ornamental bunch from the azalea family; finally the branch with very narrow leaves, dark green above and silvery below, is a willow-leaved sea buckthorn. The colours of the asters are unbelievably beautiful, the whole bouquet a genuine autumn painting. I am very pleased to know that the old man [Franz Mehring] is already better. He is one of those large trees that like a small child collapse right away with the slightest illness but get up again just as fast. Yesterday I received a letter from Karl [Liebknecht]. In every respect his situation seems wretched, though he writes cheerfully as always and at least was in good health at the time; the letter was already written on the 25th and how it is with him

since then only the gods know. He has received my card and I will very soon give him my news. I also had a line from Clara [Zetkin].

But why do you write today so colourless and sad? Has something happened or does my ear deceive me? I hope you will immediately let me know everything you learn, whether good or bad; the worst is the uncertainty. How is Grozi [Leo Jogiches]? Has he given up his work again or is he lacking energy?* You were going to teach him to be more lively. As usual I have a few requests: 1) a cup! and if possible with the same pattern: palm leaves. 2) the second book of Tugan-Baranowsky (*Theoretical Foundations of Marxism*), in my flat on the big bookshelf. All this can wait of course till the next opportunity. Still a little disquiet bothers me. Are you giving a proper account to my cashier and noting all the countless expenses?! I'd be very happy if you could put my mind at rest.

Many thanks for the cherries, they are a masterpiece. And thanks to you I'll have a festive dinner this evening.

I embrace you and Mimi heartily,
      Yours R.

I've just noticed a completely new belt on my skirt. What a magician you are that everything rejuvenates in your hands! But why waste your time and attention on such wretched trifles? This makes me quite unhappy. [...]

<In February 1915 when Rosa Luxemburg started her one-year prison sentence, it seemed infinitely long to me to have to live through that year . Was not every hour a deprival of freedom in a narrow prison cell in which light filters only gloomily through the barred window? Life is so poor in prison, it must destroy the strongest body and wear out the most resistant nerves.> At last the year in prison was coming to an end. Rosa Luxemburg's flat was in formidable order. Leo Jogiches was satisfied. During the 'great clean-up' he did not at any time cede the role of chief inspector, making sure that each object was in its old place.

Rosa Luxemburg was to be freed exactly to the hour that she had been taken into prison, at 3.30 p.m. She had asked me to fetch her and accompany her home. When I told Karl Liebknecht, who was on leave in Berlin to attend the sessions of the Prussian parliament, he wanted to accompany me. I knew him to be unpunctual and threatened not to wait. But when I arrived before time at Potsdamer Platz, the place of our appointment, Karl Liebknecht was already waiting for me with as many flowers in his hands as he could hold.

* This refers to the publication of the Junius pamphlet.

Much too early we took a taxi and went from café to café, ordered something but were too excited to consume it. Moreover we were concerned as to how the planned demonstration would come off. The socialist women of Berlin did not want to forgo greeting Rosa Luxemburg on leaving prison. As they feared that the police would put up road blocks, some of them had hidden in the houses in Barnim-strasse and the adjoining side streets since the early hours of the morning. The police did indeed cordon off the streets leading to the prison when they saw a procession of demonstrators arriving. The demonstration then went into Friedrichshain park close by. But the comrades who had hidden themselves leapt out when our car approached the prison and cheered Karl Liebknecht so that the police were powerless for the moment.

With all this excitement and under the impact of the expressions of sympathy, when I got to the prison I forgot to go to Rosa Luxemburg until the supervisor came and asked me if I did not want to take Frau Dr Luxemburg home. 'You enquired about the time of release in such a harmless way,' she added. 'I could not have dreamt that such nonsense would be organised. The women would be better occupied mending their husbands' socks and doing the housekeeping.'

Finally I was standing before Rosa Luxemburg. 'Don't you want to take me home, Mathilde? You have been here so long and haven't come to me. We're waiting for you so that we can drive home.' Adolph Hoffman[28] had joined us and brought his comrade a bunch of red carnations. Answering her questions as to how he was, he replied in his original manner: 'I'm well, Rosa. Five doctors in the hospital couldn't cure me to death.' The supervisor asked us to leave the prison by the infirmary exit in Weinstrasse which was not occupied by people and arranged for the car to wait there. We crossed the infirmary yard. The infirmary cells there have somewhat larger windows, not below the ceiling as with the prison cells but at a normal height. From all these little windows the inmates looked through the bars and waved with handkerchiefs; wardresses looked out of the corridor windows; the prison was in tumult, excited and torn from its wretched grey monotony.

Karl Liebknecht wanted the car to take us to Friedrichshain. We asked him to refrain from this as we feared Rosa Luxemburg could be arrested once more. So we drove directly to Südende. <None of us thought of paying the driver and so the car remained waiting outside the house. Friends and deputations from the Berlin constituencies came to greet Rosa Luxemburg. They all brought presents as a sign of welcome. Soon the flat resembled both a green-

grocer's shop and a grocer's. Again the bell rang. The driver: 'Are the ladies and gentlemen coming down?' 'Oh God, what is the taxi doing here?' In the meantime the fare had gone up considerably. We had to pay 20 Mark.>

Telegrams of greetings and sympathy arrived, friends and deputations from the Berlin constituencies arrived with flowers and gifts. These were quite precious given the period and consisted of flour, rice, semolina, preserves or whatever the women had saved for their beloved leader, so that she could at least live more comfortably during the first few months. 'Mathilde,' Rosa Luxemburg said that evening, 'you must think who I can give some of the food to.' She did not want to keep so much for herself whilst others suffered deprivation. When she was in bed, tired but contented, she said, thinking probably of her comrades in suffering: 'Oh, why is everything all right just for me?'

Karl Liebknecht and family

2. Five Months of Freedom

Though thorough rest was indicated, Rosa Luxemburg worked without any relaxation. Often she wrote her manuscripts whilst in heavy pain. When I said: 'Rosa, perhaps you should have a little rest,' she answered: 'I take no notice of the pain. I act as if it doesn't concern me and then I can work very well.' I frequently stayed the night in Südende. The flat had a pretty guest room which Rosa Luxemburg arranged for me. I mostly took care only that the other rooms were in order, and spent little time tidying my own room. One day I discovered it thoroughly cleaned, some new books on the table and flowers in vases and baskets. 'Yes,' said Rosa, 'I scrubbed and polished the room, I know how to do that. My prison cell was as clean as a jewel box.'

At that time Leo Jogiches and Karl Liebknecht were the most frequent guests at Südende. Sometimes Sonia Liebknecht[1] accompanied her husband. These were pleasant hours, politics was banned and after brief conversation we would recite aloud, mainly from Goethe.

For some years Karl Liebknecht had called on me for support work. I admired his courage and perseverance, and treasured his manner which was always calm, friendly and comradely. <Whether Karl Liebknecht had much or little to eat, he shared it with us. If we went to his flat to carry on working, usually late at night, there would be all kinds of dishes on the table — fish, herring, meat, vegetables; everything was cold and ready to eat, and we enjoyed it. One evening he passed me some swedes for a second time. 'Please take some more of these, they are excellent.' 'Thank you, I don't want any more.' 'Oh, you mean because they are cold; that is a prejudice, they taste very good.'

Karl Liebknecht generally ate sausages complete with the skin. When he later on returned from penal servitude he likewise ate potatoes with their skin. He had become used to this in prison, he replied to my astonished exclamation; this way he filled up more quickly. One day a Russian doctor was waiting for Karl Liebknecht when he came home. He was asked to eat with them, took a herring dish and helplessly looked around. 'Do you want another plate?' 'Yes, please.' Karl Liebknecht handed him a plate from a cupboard.

The doctor was still looking around. 'Is anything else missing?' 'If I could have a clean knife and fork.' 'Please, here it is, but you are terribly spoiled!' If we went to a restaurant Karl Liebknecht scrutinised the prices and chose the cheapest dish, generally stewed meat. His father had done likewise, and I was surprised to see the same with his eldest son Wilhelm when I occasionally ate with him in a restaurant. This did not mean that when Karl Liebknecht was in funds he could not order a refined good meal.

The close co-operation between Karl Liebknecht and Rosa Luxemburg commenced, as already mentioned, at the outbreak of war. Without being clear what exactly my fears were, I wished that Karl Liebknecht were less inseparable from Rosa Luxemburg, but saw that my wishes were in vain. Karl Liebknecht's political significance, moreover, grew beyond him. His name became inseparable from Rosa Luxemburg's, which gave him intellectual standing. His political interventions became more and more courageous and intrepid. Frequently his actions were quite foolhardy and not without vanity. If Franz Mehring or Rosa Luxemburg begged him to refrain from this or that action he used to reply that we should not worry about him, his immunity as a member of parliament would protect him from arrest.> Occasionally I spoke with Rosa Luxemburg critically about Karl Liebknecht, and she replied: 'Don't compare him with Leo Jogiches, as you always do. Compare him with the German comrades and you will see how high above them he stands. Besides, you should read Lassalle thoroughly. You can learn a lot from this; he too was vain.' She herself knew her Lassalle and loved him.

Rosa Luxemburg greeted every new spring with delight. But that spring [1916] after she had left the narrow prison cell, the new leaves and buds filled her with particular joy, and she was jubilant at drawing the first speedwell from its hiding place. After a walk with Karl Liebknecht she said to me: 'I didn't know that Karl was such a good botanist. The poor chap has until now always lived *ventre à terre*, I'll be able to cure him of this.' Sometimes Rosa Luxemburg and I travelled early in the morning to lovely Lichtenrade. On occasion Leo Jogiches accompanied us. Rosa Luxemburg had prevailed *vis-à-vis* Leo Jogiches to the extent that she did not let herself be deprived of the enjoyment of walks and visits to the theatre or concerts. One of her declared favourites was Mozart. With great enjoyment she listened repeatedly to *The Marriage of Figaro*. She very much loved Hugo Wolf's settings of Goethe's poems; she read and collected everything which appeared about Wolf.

Several times she travelled to illegal meetings across the country, to give talks about the political situation. The subsequent discussion led to the clarification and political understanding of the audience. It gave Rosa Luxemburg pleasure to regain personal contact with party friends. She returned very satisfied from a journey to south Germany. In Stuttgart she had stayed some days with Clara Zetkin. It was the last time the two saw each other. <'It was nice to be in a properly managed household,' Rosa Luxemburg said on her return. Also her friend Hans Diefenbach, who I will speak of later, she saw for the last time in Stuttgart during this journey.>[2]

She also visited Paul Levi. He was in Königstein-im-Taunus, ill from a war injury. As requested by Rosa Luxemburg, I sent him the Junius pamphlet immediately on its publication. 'The first book that I read again,' he wrote, 'my strength was insufficient until now. But I read this right through without putting it down. It is great.'

<Another time Rosa Luxemburg returned home from the beautiful town of Brunswick excited and happy. As soon as she entered the room she asked me to hand her Mörike's poems: 'Listen, Mathilde, Mörike's works are going around my head.[3] Oh, Mathilde, why didn't you come with me to Brunswick? You would have been pleased at the way the comrades cheered after my lecture. I did ask you to come; I knew what I was doing.'

In the years before the war Rosa Luxemburg had a comfortable household with an employee to do the necessary work,[4] but she had to let her go now and be satisfied with an hourly help; her regular income stopped. The teaching at the party school had covered Rosa Luxemburg's living costs. At the beginning of the war the school was closed; what need was there for scientific socialism, which didn't even provide arguments for the political truce! It was the same with Rosa Luxemburg's articles. They were not written in the timbre of political truce, and the few Social-Democratic newspapers which would have liked to print them were forbidden to do so by the censorship. Little Rosa was 'poor as a church mouse', as she herself expressed it once. She had no savings. The little money that she had left went on books.>

The all-German illegal conference of the Spartacus group, held in Berlin on 1 January 1916, decided to step up political activity. The delegates accepted six guidelines as their political platform. These guidelines, which represented an application of the Erfurt programme of international socialism to the problems of the day, were drafted by Rosa Luxemburg, and one or other of them served from then on as a motto at the head of pamphlets and leaflets. These guidelines appeared for the first time in print as an appendix to the Junius pamphlet.[5]

As the first major action of the Spartacus League a demonstration was prepared. Not all of the Arbeitsgemeinschaft[6] took
part. Some of its leaders were amongst the demonstrators, others
appeared as spectators on a café balcony, while a third group had
rejected the demonstration. But many workers showed up, which
was what mattered. They were summoned in the factories by handbills
with the following text:

For 1 May, 8 p.m.
All who are against the war will turn out on 1 May at 8 o'clock in
the evening in the Potsdamer Platz (Berlin).

<The First of May 1916 approached. The Spartacus group had
prepared a demonstration for this day. The leaders of the Independent
Socialists had refused to participate in this. But many workers were
not in agreement and joined the demonstration in large numbers
against the decision of their leaders. In spite of a unanimous feeling that Karl Liebknecht had no right to expose himself to danger, he could not be persuaded from joining the masses. In these
circumstances Rosa Luxemburg also joined the demonstration. On
1 May they both appeared at the assembly point of the demonstration in Potsdamer Platz.> 'Down with the war! Down with the
government!' Karl Liebknecht repeatedly called to the crowd.

Suddenly I noticed Rosa Luxemburg and Karl Liebknecht being escorted by policemen. I also saw how the police were beating
people with rubber truncheons and I heard indignant shouts: 'Aren't
you ashamed at beating a helpless person?' Karl Liebknecht was
taken to the police post at the Potsdam railway station and Rosa
Luxemburg went along voluntarily. I managed to follow them to
the door of the police station. After a short time Rosa Luxemburg
approached me with the words: 'Here I am, Mathilde.' 'But you
wanted to be arrested, Rosa. Have they let you go? Where is Karl?'
'Please come, we are demonstrating now. Karl is still in the police station, but he has immunity as a deputy, he'll come soon.'
We mingled among the demonstrators while the police attempted
to disperse the crowds. The road was filled with mounted police
who drove their horses into the crowds. But the people stood up
to them valiantly and repeatedly started singing revolutionary songs.

After the police had managed to drive the demonstrators into
the side streets so that the procession was forced to break up we
went to the *Vorwärts* editorial offices to ask party friends to demand that the police release Karl Liebknecht. But we found nobody
able to help us. Finally we reached Hugo Haase on the telephone.
He accompanied us to the Alexanderplatz prison, as we had found

out that Karl Liebknecht had been brought there. By now it was midnight and no information was given in the prison at night. Tired and exhausted we went home. Early next morning Rosa Luxemburg went to Sonia Liebknecht to inform her of her husband's arrest. As usual Karl Liebknecht had locked his study and while the pair were discussing how they could get into the room to remove any-thing 'compromising', two detectives appeared. The room was broken into by force and the remaining May Day handbills were requisi-tioned. The text of this leaflet, which Rosa Luxemburg had writ-ten, read as follows:[7]

Forward to the May celebration

> 3) The centre of gravity of the organisation of the proletariat as a class is the International...
> 4) The obligation to carry out the decisions of the International takes precedence over all else...

Comrades!
For the second time the First of May rises over a bloody sea of mass murder. For the second time the world holiday of labour finds the proletarian International beaten into ruins whilst the fighters of people-liberating socialism slaughter each other as unresisting cannon fodder.

For two years the Socialist International has been on its knees, and what have the workers of all countries, what have the peoples won? Millions of men have already given their lives at the bourgeoisie's behest, millions have been turned into wretched cripples for the rest of their lives. Millions of women have been widowed, their children orphaned, millions of families have succumbed to irreparable suffering and mourning. Not enough! Misery, inflation and famine rule Germany, France, Russia and Belgium, while Poland and Serbia, which the vampire of German militarism has sucked dry of blood and marrow, resemble large cemeteries and deserts of ruins. The whole world, and renowned European civilisation, drowns in the unleashed anarchy of the world war.

And to whose use and profit, to what purpose, is all this terror and bestiality? So that the East Elbian Junkers and the profiteers allied with them can fill their pockets by subjugation and exploitation of new countries. So that the sharks of heavy industry, the army suppliers of the bloody battlefields can drag a harvest of gold into their barns. So that stock-exchange jobbers profiteer with war loans. So that food speculators get fat at the cost of the hungry people. So that militarism, the monarchy, the blackest reaction in Germany can rise to a power and undivided domination never before reached.

The working class allows itself to be driven like a herd of sheep to the slaughterhouse to make its worst enemy strong and arrogant. And the bloody orgy does not stop there, it extends ever further! Tomorrow perhaps the genocide will stretch to new countries and parts of the globe. The German warmongers are using all their power to provoke war with the United States. Tomorrow perhaps we'll be told to draw the sword against new brothers, against the breasts of our American comrades in work and struggle.

Workers! Party comrades! Women of the people! How long will you watch quietly and undisturbed this spectre of hell? How long will you suffer silently the crimes of butchery, need and hunger? Be aware, as long as the people do not move to express their will, the genocide will not cease. Or perhaps it will cease when all countries have been turned into beggars, when all peoples are annihilated and nothing of so-called civilisation is left standing. The rich can still 'hold out' for a long time. They do not suffer hunger, they have hoarded plenty of supplies, and their business is flourishing nicely with the slaughter, they strengthen their political domination by the suicide of the working class. But we, the working people of all nations, how much longer do we want to continue to forge our chains with our own hands?

Workers, party comrades, enough of the fratricide! The First of May arrives as a warning voice, it knocks at your hearts, at your conscience. The betrayal of socialism, of the international solidarity of the workers, has thrown the peoples into the destruction of the world war. Only a return to the gospel of people-liberating socialism, return to the proletarian International, can save civilisation and the workers' cause from the abyss. So show then on the First of May that this gospel lives in your hearts and heads. Prove to the ruling classes that socialism and the International are not dead, that they rise with new vigour like a phoenix from the ashes! The proletarian International cannot be re-established by a few dozen people in Brussels, Bern or The Hague. It can only arise again by the action of millions. It can only arise again in Germany as well as over there in France, in England, in Russia if the masses of the workers on all sides grasp for themselves the banner of class struggle and make their voice heard like thunder against the genocide.

Workers, party comrades, women of the people! Do not let this second May Day holiday of the world war pass without forming it into a proclamation of international socialism and a protest against the imperialist butchery.

On the First of May we reach out a brotherly hand across all frontiers and battlefields to the people of France, Belgium, Russia, England, Serbia, the whole world! On the First of May we call with thousands of voices, 'An end to the war! We want peace! Long live Socialism! Long live the workers' international! Proletarians of all countries, unite!'

Based on this leaflet, many thousands of which had been handed out, and because he was 'caught red-handed' in the words of the emergency law regarding the immunity of deputies, Karl Liebknecht was taken from Alexanderplatz to the prison in Lehrterstrasse and proceedings started against him. Difficult days now began for Rosa Luxemburg. She had to take on a large part of the political work carried out by Karl Liebknecht. She was a great help to Sonia Liebknecht and made every effort, by bringing books for the prisoner, to help him forget the dreariness of prison. She conferred with Theodor Liebknecht,[8] Karl's brother, about the legal steps to be taken.

The first day of the trial in July 1916 already brought the verdict — not unexpectedly: two-and-a-half years' penal servitude! On this day the Berlin workers demonstrated and struck for their Karl Liebknecht. Shop stewards of the Ad Hoc Working Group and the Spartacus League who had agitated for this in the factories were imprisoned or sent to the trenches. Karski, and after him the aged Franz Mehring, had been arrested earlier on. Rosa Luxemburg replied to this with a leaflet which was distributed over the whole of Germany as well as at the front:[9]

Two-and-a-half Years' Hard Labour!

Workers! Party comrades!
  The blow has fallen. They have convicted our Karl Liebknecht to two and a half years' hard labour. Because he cried: 'Down with the war!' the warmongers sent him to prison. Because he demonstrated on 1 May for fraternisation of nations, he is to starve in the house of the depraved. Because he fought for bread and freedom for the people they have put him in chains.
  Comrades! Will we accept this shameful judgment quietly? Will we tolerate this bloody kick in the face?
  Workers! Women of the people!
  Leave the factories!
  A powerful protest strike across the whole country will show the sabre dictatorship that the German people no longer cower like dogs. We are fed up with the genocide and its horror! We are fed up with scarcity, hunger and the iron collar of the state of siege. The rulers shall learn that hundreds of thousands, millions stand behind Liebknecht, and like him cry: 'Down with the war.' This call will echo across the whole country like thunder and reverberate in the trenches. We will then see if the executioners dare to uphold their shameful verdict. Once again, working men and women, come out and strike in protest! Long live the prisoner Liebknecht! Down with the war! [...]
  You hold us back but you do not subdue us! The German workers have woken up! The stone has started to roll. The struggle

is not finished with this first protest strike. Workers, prepare yourselves for new action. The police truncheons can drive you from the street, but no power on earth can force you into the workshops! Long live Liebknecht! Down with the war!

After the appeal in August 1916 brought an even more draconian verdict, the workers in the factories were again called to protest strike action. Leaflets with the following text were distributed:[10]

Workers! Class comrades!
    Karl Liebknecht, the courageous, fearless fighter for workers' liberation, for peace and humanity was sentenced on August 23rd to four years and one month penal servitude, and six years' loss of civil rights. This shameful bloody sentence is a measureless challenge, a kick in the face to the German working class. Forward to combat, forward to protest! Stop work, leave the workshops and factories.

> Wake up, man of labour,
> And recognise your power!
> All the wheels stand deadly still
> If your strong arm only will!

Long live Liebknecht! Down with the genocide! Peace, freedom, bread!
(Work is to stop from Thursday, August 31st)

The strike took place on the date fixed. A powerful demonstration of the workers protested against this class verdict. On 4 November, Karl Liebknecht appeared for the third time in court. The sentence was upheld. He was now moved from Lehrterstrasse to the penitentiary in Luckau. Once a month his wife Sonia was allowed to visit him with their children. The following letter gives a palpable image of the ordeal:

Steglitz, 11th January 1917
Dear Mathilde,
    [...] Cosiness ends at Luckau. Karl was shown to us like a wild animal or a monkey behind a high wire fence. His hair has been completely shaved off, definitely not recognisable, tense and restless. Later on this dog of a guard opened the fence so that we could say goodbye properly — until the beginning of April. The whole is an invention of the devil, a nightmare — something quite impossible and incomprehensible — you want to scream, rage until you fall down dead or I don't know what. But people withstand it — it is unbelievable but they withstand it — and this is what 'reassures' me. And besides — you can't do anything, only

wait. Tell Rosa that Karl asked after her and sends her his special greetings.

As he maintains, his health is not at all bad, even good — and that is what matters in the end.

I am enclosing a letter to Rosa. Give it to her, but only if it is possible.

Kind regards — au revoir,

Sonia Liebknecht

The Berlin political police could be in no doubt that the strike and demonstration after the Liebknecht verdict were the work of Rosa Luxemburg, but proof was lacking, and the circumstantial evidence was insufficient. Even a draft of the leaflet quoted below, found in her flat during a search, which was distributed at that time in factories and in the trenches, did not prove anything. But many brave comrades had to languish in prison for distributing it.[11]

Hunger!

3) The centre of gravity of the organisation of the proletariat as a class is the International...

4) The obligation to carry out the decisions of the International takes precedence over all else...

What had to come has happened. Hunger in Leipzig, in Berlin, in Charlottenburg, in Brunswick, in Magdeburg, in Coblenz and Osnabruck, in many other towns riots of starving crowds outside food shops. And the government of siege has only one reply to the hunger cry of the masses: a more severe state of siege, police swords and army patrols.

Herr von Bethmann-Hollweg accuses *England* of the crime of causing hunger in Germany, and the government supporters and those bent on 'holding out' repeat the line. But the German government must have known that things would turn out that way; war against Russia, France and England had to lead to a blockade of Germany. It was always the custom among noble brothers in war to cause each other economic damage, to stop the food supply. The war, the genocide, is the crime, the starvation plan is only a consequence of this crime.

The callous enemies have *'encircled'* us, sob the warmongers. 'Why did you pursue a policy which led to this encirclement?' is the simplest rebuttal to this. All predatory imperialist policy is a crime and all states pursued such a policy. The imperialist policy of the German government, moreover, was one of jostling all other states, coming into conflict with all, and finally it deliberately contrived the war, allied only with the Austrian state carcass and the hopelessly bankrupt Turkey.

On top of this criminal contrivance a further crime was added: *the government did nothing* to counter starvation. *Why was nothing done?* Because the hunger of the masses does not hurt the government associates, the capitalists, the junkers, the food profiteers, it only leads to their enrichment. Because, if serious measures to combat hunger and privation had been taken right from the beginning, the dreadful seriousness of the situation would have been understood by the deluded masses. But then their enthusiasm for the war would soon have dissolved.

That is why they dazed the masses with triumphant howls of victory while at the same time delivering them to the agrarian and capitalist food profiteers. With the cry to 'hold out', with which Scheidemann[12] and company venally served the government, the attempt was made to render the masses completely senseless. The ruling classes did not want to abandon their mad lust for annexation, and the people were lied to and told: If we hold out, Germany will dictate the peace and rule the world.

They lied to us that *German submarines* would sever supplies to England, England would beg for peace and with that the war would be over. These are fairy-tales for children. The submarine warfare only brings Germany new enemies; and cutting off supplies to England is out of the question, now or at any time, even if Germany had ten times as many U-boats.

Then they pretended that the *advance into the Balkans* would create a breathing space for Germany. Food in large quantities would come from Turkey. They lied deliberately, for anyone with any knowledge knows that Turkey cannot meet the need, that in Constantinople and the coastal towns of Asia Minor there is scarcity and that the Turkish government can no longer feed its army.

Now we are consoled with the *coming harvest.* All need will be over when the new crop is in. This too is a deliberate lie. Simple arithmetic says: in twenty-two months of war two harvests were consumed, as well as the large reserves of animal fodder, sugar and other products which were stored in the country at the beginning of the war; on top of this, all that was 'requisitioned' in the occupied territories of Belgium, northern France, Poland, Lithuania, Estonia, Serbia; finally, whatever could be imported from Holland and the Scandinavian countries. Now there is nothing left. The occupied territories have been eaten bare, in Poland and Serbia people are already dying of hunger. The neutral states seal off their exports as they themselves suffer scarcity. The domestic harvest cannot yield much, as due to lack of manpower, fertiliser and seed the land was badly managed. The stock of cattle is low.

A *'food dictator'* is supposed to ensure good distribution — too late! The food profiteers have completed their task. And it does not help grabbing them by the neck now. There is not enough to 'share out' to still the hunger of the people.

That is the naked truth.

The people were driven into the war, which led to supplies being cut off; capitalist criminals with the approval of the government have done the rest.

What *is to become?* The war can be waged for another six months, perhaps a whole year, by letting people slowly starve. But then the future generation will be sacrificed. To the terrible victims of dead and injured on the battlefield there will be further victims, children and women who due to the scarcity will succumb to disability as a result of hunger.

And even then there will be no end; this war can no longer be decided by force of arms even if it lasts one or two more years. In spite of all its 'victories', German militarism is caught in a cul-de-sac. If the war still continues it is simply and solely because the masses patiently accept this infamy.

Men and women of the working people! We all bear the responsibility. Either the working masses remain in a thick-headed indifference, the consequence of which will be long sickness or a miserable doom, or the proletariat arises, refuses service to this government and these ruling classes and enforces peace.

There is no choice. Action is what matters. Arise, you men and women! Make your will known. Make your voices heard. 'Down with the war! Long live the international solidarity of the proletariat!'

<After the verdict against Karl Liebknecht had been confirmed and carried out there was nothing more which could be done, either legally or personally. Tired and worn out, Rosa Luxemburg decided to allow herself a holiday to recuperate. The necessary preparations were discussed, and I looked forward with pleasure to accompanying Rosa Luxemburg for a few weeks to Thuringia, where she intended to take lodgings under her married name of Lübeck,[13] with a family recommended to us by party comrades. Further plans envisaged extending the journey to Clara Zetkin in Stuttgart. But it turned out differently.>

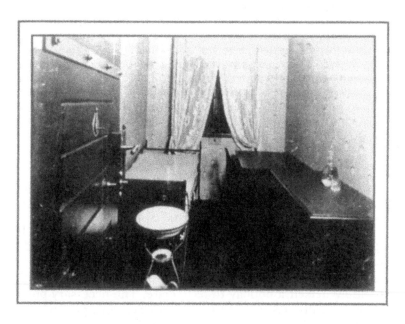

Rosa Luxemburg's room in the Wronke fortress

3. Return to Prison

During the first days of July [1916], Rosa Luxemburg was asked by Leipzig comrades to take part in their internal discussions and give some political presentations to a very restricted circle. We expected her back on 9 July. As I was walking up to her flat in the morning of that day — it was a Sunday — two men met me on the stairs. When I went to open the door they suddenly came up to me, introduced themselves as party comrades from Neukölln and asked if they could come into the flat as they had an important request to make. Then one of them, who was later to cause us some further annoyance, said he had come to commission a leaflet and had to speak to Frau Luxemburg without fail. I was surprised, as such matters were handled with much greater care and never by third persons. I asked them to entrust me with the task so that I could pass it on. This was impossible, the man claimed, he had to speak to Frau Luxemburg personally. I explained to him that I did not know when she would return, he should enquire later on by telephone so that he would not come all the way in vain.

In the afternoon Rosa Luxemburg returned. The art historian Eduard Fuchs[1] and the *Vorwärts* editor Dr Ernst Meyer[2] had met her at the station and accompanied her. I told her about the strange visitors, whom Eduard Fuchs in particular found suspicious. <Nobody however believed that Rosa Luxemburg would be re-arrested, though this was talked about in the preceding days by various people. There were so many rumours, only a fraction of which were true.> During the night Rosa Luxemburg thought over my report; she was convinced that the people I had dealt with were police spies. Early the next morning the two individuals returned and identified themselves as detectives by showing their identity cards. I was frightened, but since then no police spy has been able to take me in. The one who acted as spokesman on the previous day went immediately to the writing desk in order to search it. The request of Rosa Luxemburg that they should wait until she was dressed, as the spies had woken her up, was deliberately ignored. The spy behaved boorishly, he even wanted to force open the bedroom door, though he had seen that Rosa Luxemburg was only wearing a nightdress.

In order to quickly come to an understanding with her I brought her water and did a few other minor things. I was not allowed to answer the telephone when it rang. Bread to go with her tea I had to fetch in company of the other spy.

After breakfast I put the most essential things in a small suitcase. As it was too heavy for Rosa Luxemburg to carry, I was allowed to accompany them. We took the suburban train to Potsdam station. The officials wanted to get rid of me, so at this point they took a taxi and after four-and-a-half months of freedom Rosa Luxemburg was brought back to the women's prison in Barnimstrasse. As the government had no convincing evidence for an accusation it was unable to launch proceedings against Rosa Luxemburg. But the famous preventive custody was in force, which without further ado was exercised over a person so 'dangerous to the state'. <Rosa Luxemburg now envisaged years of imprisonment. She could count on her release only at the end of the war. She herself could not estimate how long this terrible war would last. At first the cleverest heads believed in a maximum of two years, but gradually even the wisest refrained from any such prediction. The time with its apparent hopelessness lay heavy on all.>

Conditions for prisoners in protective custody were better than for convicted prisoners. It was permitted to bring food, flowers and objects which made the cell more inhabitable. A reasonable number of letters could be written and received. My mother took it on to cook for Rosa Luxemburg according to medical prescription. We sent her lunch every day and if possible added something for the other meals. Friends also helped. <A witty six-liner of Franz Mehring from 28 July 1916 is a reminder of that time:

> The capers and the parmesan
> Taken from us by the enemy
> I did not add to the chicken;
> In spite of this think of me.
> If you do not like the war food,
> It was not I who started the war.
>
> Hearty greetings, Franz and Eva Mehring.>

Short written greetings sent in with the food generally reached Rosa Luxemburg uncensored. She also sent out with the empty dishes scraps of paper on which she wrote her requirements or brief communications. For example: 'I waited today in vain, am very sad. Bunch of clover for Lek.* Kiss. Greetings R.' 'Hay and grass

---

* Karl Liebknecht in Lehrterstrasse prison.

are for Mimi. Wine returned with thanks. Please give it to Lek. I don't drink any. Kiss.' 'The booklet disappointed me.* Kiss for Sunday.'

At Christmas words were added to little gifts: 'For my daughter Mimi and for Mathilde's mother with thousand greetings for Christmas and New Year. R.'

I had received general permission from the *Kommandantur* [military headquarters] in charge of the prisoners in protective custody to visit Rosa Luxemburg once a week. This visiting hour was at first supervised by an official sent from the central police office. One day he was replaced by the police spy who had behaved so badly during Rosa Luxemburg's arrest. At first he allowed one hour's conversation but he always behaved provocatively. He lounged on the chair and observed us with insolent looks so that we found it difficult to keep to the subject. I heartily wished to be free of this informer and did not think that the *Kommandantur* would always go to the trouble of sending an official from the police headquarters. For we talked only about private matters — friends, books, theatre or other harmless events. In the last visiting hour but one that this spy spent with us, I had brought Rosa Luxemburg a rose which she put in water. She also handed me a glass of water for some grass which she had picked for me in the yard. At this point the spy opened his big mouth and said it was not good manners to put flowers into drinking glasses, a prisoner had to comply strictly with the house rules. Rosa Luxemburg as usual did not reply to him. She had also asked me never to respond. With difficulty we pulled ourselves together, experiencing the spy's behaviour as a psychological torture. On the day before each visit I felt depressed and wondered if it would not be better to renounce it and make a complaint.

When this spy was again present at the visiting hour — it was to be the last with him — Rosa Luxemburg looked at her watch at the beginning and said to me she wanted to check the time in order not to be short-changed. After about ten minutes, when she was in the middle of a sentence, the spy jumped up with a violent movement and shouted at us in a sergeant-major tone: 'The visiting hour is finished.' We were frightened and assumed we should not have chosen the subject of the conversation which we had started. We were talking about the criminal process to be instigated in Düsseldorf in respect of the publication of *Die Internationale*, against all who collaborated in it. This periodical, of which only one issue could be published during the war (No.1), appeared simultaneously in Switzerland and Germany. Its authors, Rosa Luxemburg,

* No secret information was smuggled in it.

Clara Zetkin, Franz Mehring and others, expressed the strongest criticism against the German conduct of the war. This edition was distributed in large numbers without having been submitted to the censorship. 'Oh no,' said Rosa Luxemburg calmly, 'I have to discuss a matter of great importance to me and I shall continue the conversation to its end. Please remain until then.' The police spy now made such a row that the supervisor hurried in. She tried to persuade the man to remain; he was also rude and impolite to her. To a remark of Rosa Luxemburg, he said sarcastically: 'Here you have to behave well and do what you're told.' At this she lost her temper and shouted: 'You dirty spy!' Most likely he had waited for such a remark, and immediately said to the supervisor, 'You heard that, I have been insulted.' 'Yes,' said Rosa Luxemburg, 'and rightly so.' He continued further with shameless insults and in rage Rosa Luxemburg threw into a corner a bar of chocolate which had been brought to her. <The insolent remarks of the official went on and on so that Rosa Luxemburg threw a slab of chocolate at him and finally called out in agitation: 'One cannot expect better behaviour from a dirty spy.'>

By virtue of his office a Prussian official is never in the wrong, and this scene had unpleasant consequences for Rosa Luxemburg. The same day, late in the evening, she was transferred 'as punishment' from Barnimstrasse prison to the police prison at Alexanderplatz. Here she remained for about four weeks in a small and dirty cell with the mainline and suburban trains rolling by nonstop, often drowning out the noise of the city streets. There was no courtyard for the female prisoners' customary exercise. I had to take back the food which I had brought along, and order self-catering from a prescribed restaurant where the food was expensive, bad, and harmful for Rosa Luxemburg. All efforts to help her were in vain.

She wrote leaflets and articles for the *Spartakus Briefe** in the poor light which filtered through a dull pane of glass in the cell door. The cell itself was unlit. 'You see,' said Leo Jogiches, 'that is Rosa! There are no obstacles for her.' 'Poor little thing,' he added. 'How she has to suffer again now.'

We soon made sympathetic contact with the governor of the

---

* The *Spartakus-Briefe* [Spartacus Letters], at first called *Politische Briefe*, were illegally distributed during the war and eagerly read. They were originally duplicated from typewritten originals, and signed with the pseudonym 'Spartakus'. Most of their articles stemmed from Rosa Luxemburg's pen, with occasional contributions from Paul Levi, Karl Liebknecht, Julius Marchlewski, Franz Mehring, Ernst Meyer and others.[3]

Alexanderplatz prison, a middle-aged man. The new prisoner interested him. 'She is writing her autobiography,' he told me one day when I was in his office. I could not make clear to him that Rosa Luxemburg was translating *The Story of My Contemporary* by Vladimir Korolenko from Russian into German.[4] She had started this work to earn money for when she was released. The agreed fee of 2000 Mark was paid by the publishers in mid-January 1919; Rosa Luxemburg was no longer there to receive it. The greater part of her things were left unpacked in the Barnimstrasse prison on her sudden departure. After a few days Rosa Luxemburg wrote to me:[5]

> the?? (I've lost track of the date)
> My dear Mathilde!
> Yesterday there was a phone call from Barnimstrasse that my things must be cleared out, as the room is required. Please be so good as to go there *straight away* and pack all my belongings into a suitcase. Perhaps permission will be given that the packed things can be stored there somewhere until a later date.
> A further *urgent* request: please do not go to the *Oberkommando* or the *Kommandantur*.[6] Do not ask for anything or request anything for me, that is my firm wish.
> Many greetings, your
> Rosa Luxemburg

When I brought underwear and books to the prison in the last days of October I was taken to the governor. Quite shocked, he informed me that Rosa Luxemburg had been taken early that morning to Wronke. He could not even say with certainty if he had the name of the town correct. I ascertained that there was a little town with that name in the province of Posen.[7] I immediately rushed to the *Kommandantur*, to the *Oberkommando*, but nowhere did anyone admit knowing anything about it. I was told to be patient, Frau Luxemburg would write and express her wishes. <All letters to Rosa Luxemburg went via the *Kommandantur*, so that with the usual speed of dispatch news took at least eight to ten days. And Rosa Luxemburg had not the clothing she needed, no linen and also no money.> On 31 October 1916 we got news from her, that she had been transferred to the fortress at Wronke and we should send everything necessary there. A letter followed on 5 November:[8]

My dear Mathilde,

[...] It is no use sending letters to me here, they are sent back to Berlin. Please address them to: 'The Royal Kommandantur, Berlin', with an inner envelope, unsealed of course, to me, Central Prison, Wronke. Please also tell the others. Today I was informed of an entirely new order from the *Oberkommando*. Not only letters but all books which I receive or return must go via the Berlin *Kommandantur*. At this rate I will not be able to carry out any serious scientific work, which is all I could do here. Furthermore I am only allowed to subscribe by post to *one* newspaper, which is likewise an incomprehensible new regulation. I have raised objection to both new rules, perhaps it will be possible to effect a change. If for example my whole encyclopedia has to make the double journey from Wronke to Berlin, imagine the loss of time, money and ruin of the books! I hope I shall be able to see you soon [...]

Yours, RL

'Go and visit Rosa, Mathilde,' Leo Jogiches said, 'and take her the most essential things. She will be pleased, in fact she will expect it.' Leo Jogiches was convinced that the governor of a provincial prison would be allowed to act on his own initiative and would certainly let me talk with Rosa Luxemburg without advance permission from the *Kommandantur*. And indeeed this was how it turned out. 'I had hoped that one of you would immediately come to Wronke to look after me,' Rosa Luxemburg said when I visited her for the first time in her new domicile.

I had gone to Barnimstrasse to pack all the things left behind. I carefully examined each piece. Amongst them I discovered a political situation report which Leo Jogiches had dictated to me and I had smuggled in to Rosa Luxemburg. Leo Jogiches had added at the end some caring words, personal expressions of affection were so rare for him. I was pleased that this heavily incriminating document had escaped the supervisor. 'So as to ensure an impeccable control I have looked through everything personally,' she told me on handing over the belongings. The double check on my part saved all concerned from bad consequences.

The following event was characteristic of this supervisor, who was convinced that everything in her prison was in apple-pie order, that the prisoners never spoke a single word with each other and that all other draconian regulations were adhered to. The wife of the Belgian finance minister was interned in Barnimstrasse prison for some months at the same time as Rosa Luxemburg.[9] Of course, nobody was allowed to talk to the prisoner. The Belgian had found out from the guards which window was that of Rosa Luxemburg's cell; she whistled a few notes of the *Internationale* in front of it when the opportunity arose, and Rosa Luxemburg joined in. When there was a shortage of staff, the two prisoners were able to take their 'exercise' together, supervised by one guard. The two women talked together, which the official was not supposed to allow. The minister's wife was released to Belgium, where a newspaper reported her encounter with Rosa Luxemburg, and a German paper which translated this account subsequently came to the supervisor's attention. She went to Rosa Luxemburg in a rage: 'It's unbelievable how the foreign newspapers lie. You, Dr Luxemburg, are supposed to have had a conversation with Madame [de Wiart], who does not speak a word of German; it was impossible to talk to her!' That Rosa Luxemburg spoke French was more than the supervisor could imagine.

After the *Oberkommando* in Posen had given me permission to visit Rosa Luxemburg, I travelled to Wronke in mid-November 1916. The little town, literally 'Crow's Nest', lies one hour by train from the town of Posen. It is part of the Polish territory occupied by Prussia and has again become Polish after the World War. I visited for the first time a country annexed by Prussia. The thin layer of German inhabitants consisted mainly of civil servants, teachers and business people. They were hated by the Poles. Forced to speak German by attending German schools, they talked Polish amongst themselves and with their children. When they started school the teacher had to start by teaching them German. I felt like an interloper in these surroundings.

On my arrival at Wronke I went straight from the station to the prison. The public prosecutor of the little town, Dr Dossmar,[10] had taken over the office of prison governor during the war. He was a humane man, widely knowledgeable, who attempted to look after the welfare of the prisoners. The supervisor of the women's prison was Frau Else Strick. She at once recognised that Rosa Luxemburg was an extraordinary person and admired the equanimity with which she bore her fate.

At the first visiting hour Dr Dossmar was present as well as Frau Strick. It took place in the 'consulting room', a narrow whitewashed room the rear of which, about two square metres, was divided from the rest by a thick concrete barrier. This is where the prisoners were brought when they had visitors. We embraced across the barrier as best we could. Starved for news, Rosa Luxemburg whispered: 'Haven't you brought anything from Leo?' I pushed a note into her hand while the supervisor and the governor were falling over each other to make way for one another into the 'consulting room'. We then discussed everything essential from notes made in advance, and after arranging everything which I had to deal with the first visit was over. 'But,' said Rosa Luxemburg, 'you have not brought me any flowers. And I was looking forward to them so much.' 'Oh, Rosa, I've come directly from the train. I thought I might find a nursery on the way, but there are only two, both in the opposite direction outside the town. As soon as I've left my things in the hotel I will get flowers for you.' 'But this is an awful room,' I said to the governor after Rosa Luxemburg had been led away. 'If you find it so awful, we will have the visiting hour to-morrow in the supervisor's office.' I accepted this with pleasure and took leave, rather content that Rosa Luxemburg had landed on her feet so well.

Some little Polish boys who were loitering in the street offered me their services and showed me the way to the hotel. The landlord and his wife were friendly and helpful. Rosa Luxemburg received her meals from them, which considering the prevailing conditions were quite good. But dietary food was out of the question, and the hotel was not notably clean. The main reason for this was that about a hundred captured Georgians were lodged in the large dance hall. At 5 a.m. I was woken up by the clanking of two hundred wooden clogs. The prisoners were then taken to the forests to fell trees. The guards, some fifteen men, were also lodged in the hotel. A doctor whom the prisoners could consult had two rooms there, so that only one or two were left for the guests. This was sufficient for the time, as commercial travellers who used to stay at the hotel had stopped travelling because of the lack of goods. The landlord was richly compensated for this shortfall by the billetting.

The town's dignitaries met most days in the wine bar: the local judge, the public prosecutor, the director of a treacle factory and the rest. The owner of a pharmacy, a Pole, disliked these meetings and came only by express invitation. I also took my meals in this room and heard something of their dinner talk. Primarily they discussed the news in the papers. Here as everywhere the conversation at that time turned around the war. Occasionally they laughed about Berlin — 'Now everybody gets one egg per week.' If Berliners still got a few grams of butter per week by the end of the war, the poor were no longer in a position to buy it. But the gentlemen did not worry about this.

<I decided to stay about one week in Wronke and not make the three or four visits I was allowed one after the other but always with one or two days in between, so that my visits gave Rosa Luxemburg a longer change. We also knew from habitual practice

how to exchange news without looking at each other, escaping the sharp eye of the public prosecutor.> On top of this we wrote to each other secretly, and frequently I left flowers or other trifles for her at the prison. On the banks of the Warthe grew a large number of privet bushes which at that time of the year had their black berries. The lonely prisoner liked to have some branches of these or of pines and firs from the forest.

But wherever I directed my steps I always saw the gigantic prison built of bright red brick. Right next to this colossus but within its walls stood a tiny house which had been earmarked by the Prussian government for a woman political prisoner. It had only one floor: a very small bedroom and a living room which was a little larger; the two were connected by a door. A corridor led to a small garden. The rooms were comfortably furnished, with the little garden for the sole use of the prisoner. At first, however, Rosa Luxemburg was not allowed to stay in the garden, for only three sides were surrounded by walls, not very high though high enough to make a flight impossible. The fourth side was open to the prison yard. It had to be equipped with a fence before the careful public prosecutor permitted the use of the garden. He promised to keep a lookout for suitable materials but stressed how difficult these were to obtain in wartime. Within a few weeks, however, they were there, and Rosa Luxemburg could now enjoy the little garden from early morning until about six in the afternoon. That was the end of the day in prison. The women officials who were on duty during the day were then relieved by the night staff.

Rosa Luxemburg maintained that she felt well in the new surroundings. She had made friends with sparrows, blackbirds, thrushes, finches, tits and starlings. The birds got food quite according to their taste. The little tits had bacon and pieces of fat; even nuts were provided for these gourmets, but at that time these were scarce and expensive so that I could get only very few. <Rosa Luxemburg enjoyed nuts herself. I would have sent more if I could have got hold of them, though I was certain that none that I sent would reach Rosa Luxemburg's stomach, she enjoyed much more having her little friends eat them. She had Clara Zetkin send nesting boxes, in short she did everything in her power to show her love for the animals. She joyfully told the public prosecutor of the many visitors she had without his permission.>

The prison supervisor was a tactful and kindhearted woman with a multitude of interests. When I wanted to leave the flowers which Rosa Luxemburg had asked for on the first day, late in the afternoon, Frau Strick said to me: 'Wouldn't you like to put these flowers on Frau Dr Luxemburg's table yourself? I am sure she would be more pleased with them than if I brought them.' I had not hoped for such kindness. When I entered her rooms in the fortress, the little prisoner clapped her hands joyfully and ran towards me.

The visits to the fortress building had a special charm for me. Even the public prosecutor was infected by this pleasure when I spoke of it, and he also sometimes oversaw the visiting hours there. On warm days he walked with us in the little garden, where Rosa Luxemburg always plucked a bunch of the flowers she herself had planted. The supervisor asked the public prosecutor's permission to spend some of her free time in the evening with Rosa Luxemburg. Permission was given; indeed the public prosecutor himself liked to converse with his prisoner whenever he had time. <On occasion he brought along his sister to these cosy chats, and one day with Rosa Luxemburg I saw how she had painted neatly on an egg her imagined idea of a Social-Democrat.> They even intended to keep in touch later on; both the prosecutor and the supervisor wanted to visit Rosa Luxemburg as soon as she was free again. Rosa Luxemburg always managed to have a good relationship with her prison authorities. Even people with a different point of view could not escape the charm of her personality: political opponents, public prosecutors, prison supervisors, all respected her intellectual significance, and due to this Rosa Luxemburg fared relatively well in spite of the 'Prussian' discipline.

I was shocked on my next visit in January 1917 that I no longer encountered Frau Strick in Wronke. She had not felt happy in the little town with its gossip and had obtained leave to do war work in her home town, Metz. The supervisor had not forgotten Rosa Luxemburg. She wrote me a few lines from time to time and asked me to convey her greetings to the prisoner, as due to the annoying prison censorship she could not write as she wished. <Enthusiastic about the war, she mentioned in passing that she was proud to be able to take part in this sacred struggle. Naturally her point of view divided us. But in Rosa Luxemburg's private life, which she insisted on maintaining, she did not value people according to their political opinion, she was often attracted to people of high quality by their character or knowledge. Shortly after the outbreak of the revolution, when Rosa Luxemburg was again in Berlin though living not at home but in a hotel, Frau Schrick called, as she was in Berlin for a few days. She wanted to welcome Rosa Luxemburg in her new-found freedom. We were looking forward to meeting again, and agreed that Frau Schrick should visit me at my home.

We chatted for some quiet hours about the new conditions brought
about by the revolution, without forgetting the old ones. It was
the only time that the supervisor saw Rosa Luxemburg again.>

There was no immediate replacement for Frau Strick after her
departure. On my next visit the public prosecutor presided over
the visiting hour. Occasionally he tried to bend the regulations to
our wishes. But only if he managed this without objection did he
permit little things which were really not allowed. 'Oh,' I said once
to Leo Jogiches, 'this gaoler is so decent that I find it hard to deceive him.' Leo Jogiches explained to me that it was not the public prosecutor as a person I was deceiving, but that we had to try
with all means available to get rid of the ruling corrupt and cor-
rupting government system, including the functions of the public prosecutor.

Uncensored information thus continued to travel both ways.
However the public prosecutor did not make this easy for us. We
had to strain our wits so as not to founder. When one day I was
stroking Rosa Luxemburg's hand and sitting close to her, the public
prosecutor said: 'Please promise me not to hand anything to each
other.' 'Certainly,' we said simultaneously, 'we promise.' 'But how
do you manage to confide in each other? It's long been clear to me
that that you do so.' 'That is our secret,' Rosa Luxemburg said with
a smile. Even though we laughed, our nerves were put to a serious test in Wronke. If a letter or parcel that was sent appeared suspicious
to the public prosecutor, and nearly every one did so, he had it directed
via the Posen *Kommandantur*. Then communication with me was
often broken for a long while, and Rosa Luxemburg waited in vain
for an acknowledgement, so that we spent anxious days and nights.
After a little while a new supervisor arrived in Wronke, an impoverished lady from the nobility who made a disagreeable impression.
The poor prisoners had to suffer greatly from her unkind manner;
the prison staff also complained about their new boss.

Rosa Luxemburg's complete isolation had been made bearable
for her by Frau Strick. The new supervisor however knew how to
embitter the lives of the prisoners. I was shocked by the poor state
of health in which I found Rosa Luxemburg. She was unable to
work. Though she used to ignore her physical pains, she wrote to
me secretly: 'I am suffering from mental depression. At times it
is so bad that I have serious fears.' The stomach pains occurred
again, so severely that Rosa Luxemburg often took little or no food.
She suffered tortures of loneliness and asked me to visit. When I
finally came and the public prosecutor supervised the visiting hour
— he now did this most of the time as he knew we found the new

supervisor unpleasant — Rosa Luxemburg sat on my lap, leaned her head on my shoulder and allowed tendernesses which she normally did not tolerate. She was ill and helpless. I spoke with Leo Jogiches. 'Oh Mathilde,' he said, 'I cannot bear it if things are bad for Rosa, if she is ill. And she is ill, we must help her.' Leo Jogiches knew that the symptoms were of a nervous kind, which could be relieved by external impressions.

I had discussed with Rosa Luxemburg what could be done to improve her condition. The public prosecutor proposed that I should look out for a capable doctor in Posen. A brother of Rosa Luxemburg's fellow-student and friend Dr Julius Marchlewski (Karski) lived in Posen. He recommended a doctor who was only too ready to treat Rosa Luxemburg. He made his first visit to the patient in Wronke. As he could not spare the time for further visits there, and the fees to be paid would be excessive, Rosa Luxemburg obtained permission from the *Oberkommando* to visit the doctor in Posen. This made a little change; also compliance with the medical recommendations took time and interest. Rosa Luxemburg found the doctor sympathetic and she enjoyed talking with him during her visits. If there was time left before the departure of the train — and these were very infrequent — the prisoner could go for a walk or do a little shopping. The accompanying official then waited outside the shop. According to Rosa Luxemburg he was modest and reserved; though tired, she returned to Wronke stimulated.

In this period Rosa Luxemburg was incalculably temperamental. In her agitated state she feared I might ask something from the supervisor whom she found so disagreeable. On an unexpected visit she refused to see me in the belief that I had asked [special permission] for the visit. In reality the public prosecutor had offered that I could visit her more frequently, to provide distraction and pleasure. When she refused to see me, I went for a short walk and thought about how much consideration we owed Rosa Luxemburg. On the banks of a lake in the woods I saw several white blossoms shining through the green of heart-shaped leaves; they were marsh kalla. I took off my shoes and stockings and carefully risked a few steps into the marsh to pick these flowers. On my way back I left them at the prison. When the door was opened, Rosa Luxemburg waved with her handkerchief from the little garden. I hurried to the fence. 'Are you annoyed with me?' 'Oh, how could I be!' 'I already said to Frau Doktor' — I could hear the voice of the supervisor — 'if I were Fräulein Jacob I would kindly decline such a friendship.' 'If you were Fräulein Jacob I would never consider you as a friend,' came the reply.

One day we received news that Dr Hans Diefenbach, a young doctor from Stuttgart and a good friend of Rosa Luxemburg, was coming to the garrison hospital in Posen. He had broken a leg falling from a horse as a medical officer in France. Temporarily unfit for service he was assigned after short treatment to the Posen hospital to carry out light duty there. Hans Diefenbach and Rosa Luxemburg made plans for a frequent exchange of ideas in person. But they had not considered that the Prussian authorities would find it unseemly for a military doctor with the rank of an officer to have friendly relations with a criminal. Hans Diefenbach was simple enough to believe that his officer's rank would be enough to open the Wronke prison gates to him at any time.

<I already knew Hans Diefenbach quite well, as Rosa Luxemburg liked to talk about him. She always had such interesting conversations with him that when she once accompanied her friend to the train for Stuttgart, they both failed to hear the signal for departure and Rosa Luxemburg had to remain on the train. The friends got off the train at Wittenberg and wrote picture postcards that would amuse their recipients. As soon as a train for Berlin arrived Rosa Luxemburg returned whilst Hans Diefenbach continued his journey to Stuttgart. I met Hans Diefenbach in person shortly before his departure for Posen, at the salon of Paul Cassirer, where his wife, the actress Tilla Durieux,[11] read some chapters of [Rosa Luxemburg's] now finished translation of Korolenko's *The Story of My Contemporary*. When Hans Diefenbach informed me after the recital of his plans for a visit to Rosa Luxemburg, I tried strongly to dissuade him from going to Wronke without a visiting permit. Our friend, however, was too confident. Without applying for the necessary permission from the *Kommandantur*, he arrived for a first friendly visit. The public prosecutor judged the situation more correctly, he refused Hans Diefenbach the desired meeting unless he produced written permission from the Posen *Kommandantur*. He had to return sad at not being able to complete his objective. His friend was equally sad when the public prosecutor told her of the abortive visit.> [Hans Diefenbach] was reprimanded by his military superior because he had left the Posen fortress without the necessary permission. He was also told in a less than friendly manner that it was unseemly for an officer to have relations with a 'person' like Rosa Luxemburg. Hans Diefenbach had character enough not to break off such relations. He continued to correspond with his friend and sent books or periodicals to provide the prisoner with distraction and pleasure.

Occasionally I visited our friend in the Posen hospital at the

request of Rosa Luxemburg, who knew nothing of these disagreeable occurrences. He spoke of his annoyance; it did not worry him
that he had made his promotion impossible. 'But you see,' he said,
'I would like to avoid unnecessary danger. At present I am too ill
to be sent to the front straight away. I want to postpone this as
long as possible. Not for myself — I am single and would know
how to die as much as many others. But I have a great love for my
father, and it would cost him his life if he lost me. Tell Rosa in
the secret way which the two of you use that she should not put
the name of the sender on the envelopes of her letters. It is need-
less to give the people here actual proof that we are in contact.'

Despite these vexations I spent some entertaining hours with
Hans Diefenbach. Our first walk in Posen was to the memorial of
the Polish poet Mickiewicz[12] whom Rosa Luxemburg had loved
since her early youth. <Occasionally I met our friend in Unterberg,
a beautiful place for excursions near Posen, accompanied by the
Marchlewskis, a couple who had become friendly with Hans
Diefenbach.>

Suddenly Hans Diefenbach was transferred to hospital service in Prussian Lissa, which was some two hours by train from
Wronke. Here I visited our friend in springtime, when lilac and guelder
roses were in flower. <I tried to entrance Rosa Luxemburg with
this splendour. Had she not written to me once when I had brought
her a flowering linden branch: 'You do not know what kindness
you have shown me with this.' So I took her this time flowering
lilac and guelder roses, passed on the greetings of our friend and
told her various things which we had touched on in our conversation.> After some time Hans Diefenbach's father fell ill and his
son managed to get leave to go to Stuttgart. The death of his father was the first great sorrow in Hans Diefenbach's life. From this
moment he no longer cared for his own fate. The order to return
to the Western front was not long in coming... 'How long ago it
seems,' he wrote from the front on 16 October 1917, 'since I received treasured visits from ladies in lilac-flowering Lissa...' <Luise
Kautsky,[13] who had a long-standing connection with both him and
Rosa Luxemburg, had also visited him.> As early as December
one of my letters to him was returned to me with the customary
remark: 'Fallen on the field of honour.' My dread at this news was
that much greater as I knew how painful it would be for Rosa
Luxemburg. I wrote to her immediately. She asked me not to mention
this loss ever again. She wanted to be alone with her pain.

*   *   *

But back to the summer of 1917. I was in Wronke to spend my holidays near Rosa Luxemburg, and did not go on a single walk without picking flowers for her. She was particularly pleased when I brought a flower which I did not know and she could tell me its name and explain it. Over and over again I had to report to her of cows, goats, geese and ducks. Geese in particular aroused her delight. I had to tell her about the songbirds. But I rarely recognised which bird trumpeted its song. Rosa Luxemburg recognised the bird calls and could imitate them deceptively. 'In my childhood,' she said, 'my mother told me of King Solomon who understood the voices of the birds, which seemed incredible to me, but today I understand them myself.'

My idyllic holiday came to an early end. The public prosecutor told us during the visiting hour that he had been informed by the responsible authority that Rosa Luxemburg was to be transferred to another prison. At the front a lady had been convicted to several years' confinement in a fortress. As there were in Germany only two fortresses for women, and one was already occupied, Wronke had to be placed at the disposal of the convict. We could already begin travel preparations, and if it was not expressly forbidden, he would give us the location of the new prison as soon as he knew it himself. I could then try and find out the conditions there. But he was not allowed to give us the date and time of departure. This was unnecessary, Rosa Luxemburg would let me know as soon as she had been informed. Now we had to pack quickly. With the help of a warder and some Russian [prisoners] I collected those things from the prison which Rosa Luxemburg did not want to take with her in person. <I obtained boxes for the packing of pictures, books, her crockery, a cane chair, a deck chair, and various other things. I did not believe I would be able to stow away and move everything. In addition there were the various articles of food which I had gleaned in the surroundings of Wronke: eggs, butter, honey and others. It was always with special pleasure that Leo Jogiches awaited me from Wronke. Besides news of myself and Rosa Luxemburg I brought him food. Feeding him at that time was precarious. But I also always had to prove that my family were also provided for. If he had the slightest doubt, it was only with deceit that I could let him have something.> My worries about packing were relieved by the sergeant on duty; I should leave it to him. 'I learnt everything with the Prussians, even packing.' Indeed, everything reached the new destination undamaged.

In the meantime the public prosecutor had informed us that

Rosa Luxemburg would be taken to Breslau.[14] 'If you promise me not to go on the platform I shall even tell you when Dr Luxemburg will travel and on which train.' 'No, I won't be deprived of this,' I answered. 'I shall be at the station daily for the two trains going to Breslau, noon and five in the morning.' I knew already the departure date. Rosa Luxemburg was going to let me know the time as soon as she was told. She asked me to travel with her on the same train. I advised against this as I expected trouble and furthermore it was doubtful if we could talk with each other during the journey. At noon on 22 July I was on the platform. Rosa Luxemburg arrived shortly after, accompanied by the public prosecutor and a prison guard from Breslau who was to keep watch during the journey. As a conscientious official the public prosecutor made certain that everything proceeded in accordance with the rules. Perhaps it was also a pleasant duty to accompany the prisoner. He had ordered that on that day no platform tickets were to be issued. To get on to the platform I therefore booked a ticket to the next station. The public prosecutor made the best of it and we talked with each other until the arrival of the train, which was to bring Rosa Luxemburg once again to another prison, the fourth during the war.

The following morning the sergeant on duty and some of the Russian prisoners took me and my considerable amount of luggage to the train. In Breslau I immediately went to the *Kommandantur* and asked for four visiting permits, which I was granted. Already at noon I was at the prison, much to Rosa Luxemburg's surprise. She had counted on a visit the following day. She had tears in her eyes when she was brought to me. 'Oh, Mathilde,' she said, 'the change is too terrible. I have a bare cell. I am not allowed into the yard. There is no restaurant in the town which will agree to provide meals for me. I shall perish here.' I hoped to be able to help. The new abode did not seem quite so bad. Rosa Luxemburg was no longer completely isolated but was lodged in the same building as other prisoners. The pulse of life burst through to her again. We agreed that I should get a wardrobe, a washstand and some other things. Once the pictures arrived from Wronke, a small carpet which a friend had given her, the cane chair and above all else the books, Rosa Luxemburg could manage to make the cell liveable. And instead of a spy-hole in the wall with its grating, the cell had normal windows.

<Even during her imprisonment in 1915–16, when Rosa Luxemburg was given a so-called 'mother cell' which was larger than other cells and given to expectant mothers, she had given the bare room a measure of comfort by arranging some books, her writing materials and other little things. The doctor from the Barnimstrasse

prison and the supervisor there repeatedly said how cosily the cell
was arranged, she regretted she could not show me, as this would
be against regulations. After a short time I received news from Rosa
Luxemburg in Breslau that the cell has been converted to a comfortable room, as I was able to see for myself later on. Given the
much greater number of books she had acquired while in Wronke,
the one cell proved too small for both bedroom and workroom, so
an adjoining cell was added after a little while. The use of both
was practically impossible as prison cells are not connected by doors.
If the locked-up prisoner wanted to go from one cell to the other
she had to use a bell to call the warder. The warder then appeared
to let Rosa Luxemburg out of the one cell and lock her up in the
other. Because of these difficult circumstances she gave up the use
of the second cell.>

The responsible Berlin authorities arranged for an inspection
of how Rosa Luxemburg was lodged in Breslau. The Berlin officials considered the room insufficient and advised the Breslau prison
director to connect it with the adjoining one. Now Rosa Luxemburg
was reasonably well accommodated; she had a living room and a
bedroom to furnish, and everybody who came praised the prisoner's good taste. From then on she was also allowed to walk in the
yard as much as she wished. The cell doors, however, remained
locked, so that when Rosa Luxemburg wanted to go outside she
always had to call a guard.

Procuring food in Breslau was very difficult. However, there
were villages in the surounding countryside where the Breslau inhabitants could obtain vegetables, fruit, meat and, most impor-
tantly, butter. But to find a restaurant which would take on catering
for Rosa Luxemburg proved impossible. The owners were not prepared
to supply the prison with more food for one person than the food
coupons allowed. But nobody could exist on these minute quantities without suffering severe damage to their health. What was
to be done? I had obtained the address of some Breslau party friends
who might be assumed to have the necessary courage and interest to look after Rosa Luxemburg. This was the Schlisch family,
who lived in close proximity to the prison. I did not find the head
of the family, Robert Schlisch, at home when I called. He was working
on his small allotment. But without delay the oldest boy set off
on his bicycle to give his father the news that Rosa Luxemburg
had been brought to the Breslau women's prison and his help was
required. After a short while Robert Schlisch arrived. 'Don't you
worry, for our Rosa I'll have always something to spare. As a bargeman
I often have business in Upper Silesia, and food there is not yet

scarce. Selma,' he turned to his wife, 'you will cook for her, won't you? Taking it to the prison is no problem, as it's only five minutes away.' 'Of course,' said Frau Schlisch, noticeably pleased. And she did everything within her power for Rosa Luxemburg.

<The whole family, consisting of the parents, a young daughter, two boys of about nine and five, two grandmothers — the mothers of Robert Schlisch and his wife — they all bent themselves to help the housewife, and everybody in turn did something for Rosa Luxemburg. Sometimes the five-year-old Karl looked at a delicacy and sighed: 'Mummy, old Rosa always gets something special.' But he too loved 'old Rosa', he was allowed to bring her flowers and she always had a little something for him. After a while Robert Schlisch was called up for military service with the inland waterways. His wife, who wanted to visit him, wrote that during her absence she would arrange to have other people look after Rosa Luxemburg. He replied that as much as he wanted to see her, she should not come just now. Rosa Luxemburg came first, she should take care that 'our Rosa' was fed properly.>

Already on 6 August Rosa Luxemburg wrote to me, reconciled with her stay in Breslau:[15]

Breslau, 6.8.17.

My dearest Mathilde!
[....] The boxes from Wronke arrived here on the 2nd, of course I unpacked them immediately and am already quite 'settled in'. The two rooms now look halfway human, but I fear that this won't work out and I shall have to limit myself again to one cell. Two rooms are of course nice if one has admission to them; but I am always securely locked in and to reach the other cell I must knock and get the guard to move. Apart from the fact that I dislike making demands on somebody so often, it is not possible from a practical point of view, as the guard has various tasks to fulfil and frequently is not in the section. Also from 1 to 4 she is not there at all (lunch break) and from 6 in the evening she is gone, while I am allowed to have the light on until 10. This makes everything difficult, as I am either separated from my bed where I like to lie down at times between my work or when I don't feel well, as well as from my tea kettle and my medicines, or I am separated from my desk and from the light in the evening. This is quite different from Wronke and also from Barnimsrasse where the prisoners in protective custody are only locked up at night and during the day can move about freely in the infirmary; as I said, I doubt if it will be possible with the two cells under these circumstances; it will of course be very difficult for me to live with all my things in a small cell. But this will soon become

clear, don't worry about it. One must put up with it. I've had bad stomach trouble since Friday, but I hope it will now be better, I believe it is due to the local bread which I have to get used to. Otherwise the food which the woman brings for me is very good. The specialist, Dr Oppeler, whom I've been given permission to see, is on holiday until end of August. In the meantime the prison doctors are here; honestly there is very little that can help me as my stomach rejects all medicine. But don't worry about this either. I am already feeling better [...]

Your R

The Breslau prison doctor soon developed an interest in his patient. Conversation with the elderly intellectual stimulated Rosa Luxemburg. They exchanged books. The doctor loved Goethe and was pleased to find in Rosa Luxemburg a thorough Goethe expert. The doctor obtained a reader's card for the Breslau University library, so that Rosa Luxemburg's reading requirements were to a large extent taken care of. The old gentleman was an avid opera- and theatre-goer, and told Rosa Luxemburg about the productions at Breslau's artistic venues. When I came, they looked up concert and theatre performances for me, and sometimes even obtained tickets.

The main object was for Leo Jogiches to keep his comrade informed about political events. Fearing the police, who at that time did not yet come at night but frequently during the day, I wrote the reports exclusively at night. Previously Leo Jogiches had to dictate them to me, which given his thorough manner took a lot of time. He often interrupted the work and told anecdotes or tales of old times in his and Rosa Luxemburg's life. 'Let's finish work now,' he would say for example, 'I want to tell you something about Rosa which will make you laugh. When we lived in Paris we once visited friends who lived at some distance. On the way home Rosa was tired and asked a cab driver how much it would cost to drive home. The amount mentioned was high and we could not spend so much. "Oh, monsieur," Rosa called out, "nous sommes pauvres." The driver replied, "Ce n'est pas ma faute!" This reply so amused Rosa that she sat down on the ground laughing heartily and then felt no longer tired during the walk.' <When Leo Jogiches had relaxed by telling various stories he started dictating again after midnight. Then he had over an hour's walk to his flat in Neukölln. Rosa Luxemburg, who knew his way of working, had no doubts about how his reports to her were compiled.>

It was a great comfort in Breslau that the *Kommandantur* permitted the prisoners in protective custody a monthly excursion

of a few hours, accompanied by a prison guard. Rosa Luxemburg
made the excursions with the friends who visited her. <Apart from
me, Rosa Luxemburg was visited by Sonia Liebknecht, Mathilde
Wurm, Luise Kautsky and Martha Rosenbaum, and made such
excursions with these friends.[16]> To begin with she had to get used
to life in the outside world. After the first excursions she returned
to the prison exhausted. Her nerves were so tense that she could
not sleep at night. Gradually, and particularly after the bad weather
of the 1917–18 winter, when spring came Rosa Luxemburg enjoyed
the excursions. Generally we got the car to take us to some woods,
usually the Ostwitz forest or Scheitnig with its small botanical
garden.

The visiting hours took place at first in an office. A junior lawyer
from Posen and a solicitor from Berlin took it in turns to super-
vise. I happened once to meet one of the gentlemen in the prison
before the visit, and when we encountered the governor, he asked
if we wanted to go to Frau Luxemburg. 'Frau Luxemburg is brought
to us in the office,' I replied. 'I would be pleased if we could visit
her in the cell.' 'There is no objection to this,' was his reply, and
Rosa Luxemburg's face showed astonishment and pleasure when
we came in to her. From now on, when she 'had guests' the prisoner could play host. She was in her element. Leo Jogiches, who
led a retiring life, used to say that Rosa Luxemburg was only truly
happy when she regularly had people around her. But however many
enjoyed her hospitality, only a few were close to her. These few
could rely on her. Whatever external events might separate her
from her friends temporarily, her interest and concern for their fate
did not fade.

Rosa Luxemburg's friendships with animals were also intense.
Once she kept a rabbit in her flat. She waged a bitter battle with
the other inhabitants on account of this little animal. It smelled
bad, they maintained, and was very noisy. The owner pretended
not to have noticed either of these characteristics. Only when the
landlord gave her the choice of giving up either the flat or the rabbit did she decide to give the animal away. A replacement was found
in Mimi. Once during the war, when Leo Jogiches had bought some
mincemeat for the 'little beast', as he called her, he recounted how
a woman worker who could only afford to buy a few bones had
looked at the meat. 'Why are you telling me this?' was Rosa
Luxemburg's reply. 'Don't I do everything in my power to fight
for all the poor? You shouldn't spoil my joy with Mimi.'

In Breslau Rosa Luxemburg gave some white bread, which was
very rare, to a goat which she discovered on the way to the dentist.

She never missed feeding the goat when she went that way. During the winter of 1917–18 an exhausted pigeon which could not fly any further because of an injured wing, set down on Rosa Luxemburg's cell window. She washed its wound and nursed the little animal until it could fly again. '[T]he brown pigeon,' she wrote to me in June 1918, 'which I nursed here in my cell during the winter, when it was ill, remembers my "good deed". She discovered me once when I was walking in the yard in the afternoon and now waits punctually for me each afternoon, sits next to me, puffed up, on the pebbles, and runs after me when I go round in a circle. It is comic to see this silent friendship.'[17] Soon the pigeon rediscovered the window. As it was usually open it slipped into the cell. These visits were repeated and finally the little animal came daily. Companions were also 'introduced' and feeding the pigeons gave Rosa Luxemburg much joy. 'I had to stay in bed for a few days,' she wrote in September 1918, 'then the pigeons came to me on the bed. Isn't this incredible?'[18] <I was pleased if they were there during the visiting hour, swaggered about in the cell and asked for their tribute when we consumed bread or cake. Many descriptions of the interest and care which Rosa Luxemburg devoted to animals can be found in her beautiful letters from the Wronke and Breslau prisons to Frau Sonia Liebknecht.>

Leo Jogiches, c. 1915

4. Working with Leo Jogiches

After the arrest of Karl Liebknecht on 1 May 1916 the *Vorwärts* editor Dr Ernst Meyer, whom Karl Liebknecht had enrolled for illegal work, took over the leadership of the Spartacus League. When he was arrested in August 1916 Leo Jogiches replaced him. The illegal work became both more extensive and more dangerous. The police made extreme efforts to track down the keen distributors of the pamphlets 'which were infesting the army and navy'. The number who fought against the war policy and joined the Spartacus League grew steadily. Some ended up in penal servitude due to carelessness, but if there was only suspicion without the authorities being able to prove anything, they were sent to the trenches.

Leo Jogiches had never intervened in the struggles of the German workers' movement. He had kept a distance from the life of the organisation, knew none of the German comrades except a few friends of Rosa Luxemburg, and besides these no German Social-Democrat knew of his existence. After a short time he held the threads of the illegal organisation in Berlin firmly in his hands. All the correspondence and the personal contact with comrades across the country was carried out by him. I had never known such devotion, so much personal sacrifice, as I could now observe in Leo Jogiches. He was a conspirator pure and simple. This revolutionary fulfilled his obligations without political ambition, calm and conscious of his aim. He took no breaks in his work, which he extended until late at night and not infrequently until early in the morning. He kept neither Sundays nor holidays. It seemed as if he could do without sleep and food.

Abandoned by most of the comrades who had been active before the war and shortly after its outbreak,[1] Leo Jogiches achieved something extraordinary at this critical time. His judgement on the German party comrades who were supposed to help him was devastating, in all but a few cases. If they maintained that they could not do this or that because their strength was insufficient, or used any other excuse, Leo Jogiches would say, 'You should first try and see whether you collapse. It is distasteful to work with such comrades.' But there was no one who did not esteem Leo Jogiches's character highly, and greatly admire his personal achievements. Even those who were the object of his wrath did so. Inflexible as he was with the work, his character was profoundly good. The young people were greatly attached to him. A word of praise from him made them proud and happy. 'Now, tha-at you did well.' (He prolonged the 'a' in his pronounciation of German.) At this his features brightened and he looked kindly at the person he praised. The example which Leo Jogiches gave lent strength to many and gave them the impetus to carry out the 'purposeless' work against the war. Rosa Luxemburg complained at times about the excessive severity of her friend towards others. 'But he is always right,' I commented. 'That's just it, do you know anyone else who is always right!'

When I made Leo Jogiches's acquaintance he lived in Steglitz as a Russian émigré who fought clandestinely against tsarism under the name of Crystallowicz, a citizen of Lemberg [Lvov] whose papers he had. This was without danger as long as Lemberg was occupied by the Russians and the Lemberg citizens living in Berlin had no contact with their home town. But when this was reconquered by Austria there was a danger that Leo Jogiches could be apprehended as the double of this Crystallowicz. Thus it was necessary to get new papers. As he had obtained Swiss citizenship during his student days it should be possible with some adroitness to bring his former Swiss papers up to date, against payment of the accumulated sum due. In any case he could no longer stay in his flat in Steglitz. In February and March 1915 he had sent letters with his address to Rosa Luxemburg in prison. The criminal police immediately took an interest in the writer of these letters, searched his flat during his absence and questioned his landlady.

The attempt to lodge Leo Jogiches unregistered with party friends failed because of the fear of police fines or even the trenches. He therefore went fatalistically into the lion's den, to Rosa Luxemburg's flat in Südende. Everything went well, nobody looked for him there. A friend who had undertaken the mission brought back from Switzerland his papers which were in order according to the regulations. So often, and with so much difficulty, did he change papers and names, and if this did not succeed he often remained 'nameless' in the meantime. Now a politically sympathetic police officer was discovered in Neukölln, who carried out his registration and circumvented the formalities to be undertaken on entry into the country.

When the February revolution broke out in the tsarist empire Rosa Luxemburg wished heartily to leave prison and to go to Russia. The following report which by chance was not destroyed, gives an interesting insight into her and Leo Jogiches's mood at the time. In case of misadventure, which must always be expected, the details would not be fully understood by those not initiated. For a better understanding I have also added notes, and names for pseudonyms and signatures — marked as { }. At this time Leo Jogiches wrote to Rosa Luxemburg:

I. Your silence as a result of not forwarding the letters early June has greatly worried and even depressed me. Please, as a matter of urgency, go *immediately* and most thoroughly through all your things, books, notes, letters, scraps of paper, and destroy without mercy anything which indicates a connection with the outside world. I warn most urgently! I know from experience that in this position unexpected searches prompted by some accidental cause may be carried out on orders from outside. Consider what is at risk! I know you are extremely nonchalant and already last year had an experience with another comrade — it was Krusche {Rosa Luxemburg}. Amongst his things which were taken from the hospital {prison} were various letters of mine and also other things, and to me this is a warning also for you. {Refers to the compromising report that I had found with Rosa Luxemburg's things in the Barnimstrasse prison.}

II. As to your comment:[2] As I wrote, I consider it — and it is — objectively *absolutely harmless*, but it is not clever, as hopeless and also in this connection does not take into account that one is either Russian or German, regardless of other circumstances; and if one does not give up German nationality one cannot bring Russian into play, however understandable to anyone it may be that at such a time as *now* one might want to see one's country irrespective of German citizenship. But for the *Oberkommando* this is no *good* reason. I advise against pursuing the matter any further, and certainly not sending the birth certificate. The *[Ober]kommando* want to have the latter *only* to establish formally that you were born in *Poland*, and belong to the 'independent state', i.e. have no claim to be considered as a *Russian* (which is the case anyway, on account of your German nationality). For this very reason, your application will *undoubtedly be refused*. This was exactly how the case of one of your Polish friends was decided (at the Bonaventura) {Dr Julius Marchlewski}, who made the same application, although he is not a German citizen. So leave the matter alone. On the other hand I am in favour of using all legal means on the authorities, and *strongly* at that, to get you out, without giving anything away.

a) I am for you letting the lawyer act under the supervision of Gross {Leo Jogiches}. You know very well that Gross will not permit anything indiscreet or show you up. In such matters personal aspects and friendship have no validity for him (the 'pure Cato!').

b) I want to write a very offensive letter to the International

Bureau (Stockholm committee) in the name of the dear KPiL[3] and remind them of their duty to request you right away for the Bureau or otherwise.[4] The committee has done this already for Otto Bauer[5] (imprisoned in Russia) and for Pavlowitsch[6] (civilian prisoner in Austria), and with success (permission granted). Of course, I will add that you undoubtedly disapprove of the whole present activity of the *committee* (Conference etc.).

c) A letter with the same content to the same Bureau from the old man (Franz Mehring) in the name of the 'Internationale' group.*

d) Publicity in the press for the possible steps of the committee, so that the matter becomes public and the German authorities have to reckon with the pressure.

e) I will possibly try (only I don't know if this will be possible for technical reasons) to have an appropriate anouncement made at the General Congress of Workers' and Soldiers' Councils in Russia in June. Please do not mention any of these things. Because of delay and the risks of correspondence. I shall not act on my own, but ask our colleagues for advice.

III. As far as our position towards Stockholm and the current policy is concerned, in my opinion we must without fail introduce the following two ideas into our proclamations (and articles):

a) The slogan: 'peace without annexations or indemnities' has *nothing* inherently socialist about it, and is *not* the formula of a proletarian-socialist peace, despite the Russian Workers' Council having raised it. It is the peace formula of *an imperialist war which has gone hopelessly awry*, and in which the balance of forces rules out any military solution. Those governments which have realised this (Germany/Austria) also want the Stockholm Conference to take place, as it will undoubtedly take a stand on this formula. England and France, on the other hand, which in view of American help have not given up the hope of a military solution, are against Stockholm and refuse passports. For the Russians this slogan is only a *compromise*, their first slogan was 'forward to the international revolution in order to bring peace' (in the appeal 'To the Peoples of the World', 27 March).[7] At that point the Russians rejected *any* negotiation with the *governments*.

b) The enormous significance which is given the Stockholm Conference by the governments and the whole bourgeois world is *not* an expression of the *power* of socialism, but of its *impotence*. For in this connection the socialists have, partly consciously, partly unconsciously, taken on the role of mediators for their governments (as the governments could not or would not

* The Spartacus League was originally known as the 'Internationale Group' after the projected periodical *Die Internationale*, whose views its adherents supported.

negotiate with each other directly). In this the socialists simply
continued the policy of 4 August [1914], now making socialism
too a willing tool of the governments, i.e. carrying out the *old*
policy in a *new form* corresponding to the changed situation on
the ground (no prospect of victory and the need to escape from the
blind alley). In my opinion it is extraordinarily important to
stress both points of view, as appearances speak for the
Scheidemanns,[8] causing illusions and confusion. I request
comment and response *at some point.*

IV. The Teltow people,[9] and perhaps other districts as well,
will elect 3 delegates for Stockholm, including yourself.
Obviously not to the Troelstra conference.[10] Following F.'s
application for a pasport, the party executive (Haase, Ledebour)
were asked by the *Oberkommando* if F. was a party delegate.
Given that F. was elected by constituency associations, the
executive had to reply accordingly, and there is no doubt that the
passport will be issued. [...] As far as you are concerned, your
election is [not] yet a reason for your release. But the point is to
make a row and expose the authorities.[11] This in all haste, so that
you are released as soon as possible. I am convinced that you
would have been free a long time ago already if we hadn't been so
passive. Now we have to catch up.

V. Despite the lukewarm and depressed mood of the workers
here, and the unfavourable situation in Russia, I am still firmly
convinced that we will witness something important in the near
future if the war continues, as no doubt it will. And so it is
extremely important that you are free and able to intervene.
Already now you could have great influence.

VI. I have had a copy *Nowoje Wremja*[12] translated. The effect
is breathtaking, direct from a fairy tale, but some things very
worrying, in particular the Leninist idiocies which are popular
and in my view inclined to compromise the movement, dissolve
in chaos, and help Germany out of its predicament.* In it was a
long speech of Plekhanov at the plenary session of the Workers'
Council. The old windbag (by the way greatly applauded) boasted
about talks he had with K. K. (Karl Kautsky) and you at the

---

* Similarly forceful expressions, and still stronger ones, were current
between Lenin and his supporters and the circle around Rosa Luxemburg,
in the context of mutual and frequent criticism. But the news that came
from Russia to Germany was poor, distorted, and often false, so that Leo
Jogiches's judgement on Lenin's tactics at that time would have been more
supportive given a more exact knowledge of the situation. Rosa
Luxemburg, too, shared the view that the separate peace striven for by
Russia and signed at Brest-Litovsk would bring Germany a victorious
end to the war, unless English arms finally played the deciding role, as
she believed they would. A German victory, however, would certainly
mean a policy of violence and worst reaction, the heaviest threat to the
ideas of freedom and socialism.

Mannheim Party Congress in 1906 and what you said then. He
always has to make himself im-*por*-tant.
        Hearty greetings and handshake,
            Marie {Leo Jogiches}[13]

Leo Jogiches had predicted correctly. The army and navy in Germany were tired of fighting; letters from their relatives showed
despondency and despair, telling of hunger and poverty at home.
Less bread, no rights, new taxes, and no prospect of a speedy end
to the slaughter, as a leaflet now put it. And when Lenin took power
in Russia in October 1917, dissolved the Duma and turned the semi-
revolution of the Kerensky period into a full proletarian revolution, the revolutionary sparks spread to Germany. They ignited
the great strike of January 1918 in which the Independent Social-
Democrats* stood shoulder to shoulder with the Spartacus League.
In this strike the political events were so rapid that there was no
time for the Spartacus League to have its leaflets written by Rosa
Luxemburg. It would have been cumbersome to ask Franz Mehring
to do so. For Leo Jogiches visited him personally always alone, and
by a circuitous route. He changed bus or tram several times, on
arrival he circled the block repeatedly, and only when he was certain that no informer was following him did he go up to the Mehrings'
flat.

    Franz Mehring, called by his comrades 'the old man' for short,
admired the political vision of the conspirator, with whom he had
friendly ties. Whilst the least alteration in the printing of his
manuscripts caused the otherwise amiable Franz Mehring to erupt
into fury, he permitted Leo Jogiches to make changes which he
thought necessary. Leo Jogiches used to say of himself that the
practical work of writing and speaking did not suit him. He was a
good motor that set the machine in motion and made it run. Just
the same he could carry out this practical work when the conditions forced him, as with this strike. The leaflets written by him
were distinguished by their precise composition and concise style.
Only a few people, he said, can write leaflets. If these cannot be
kept short, they are boring and are not read. Rosa Luxemburg, he
said, was a writer of leaflets par excellence, he also attributed this
talent to Paul Levi, Karl Liebknecht and Franz Mehring.

    Leo Jogiches's January leaflets carried to the masses for the
first time the slogans:

* The Ad Hoc Working Group had formed itself into the Independent
Socialist Party in Gotha in April 1917. The Spartacus League had joined
it, while retaining its own forms of struggle.

ABOLITION OF THE 'BY THE GRACE OF GOD' PRUSSIAN
HOHENZOLLERNS !

DOWN WITH THE PRINCELY PARASITES OF THE GERMAN
MINI-STATES!

ABOLITION OF THE THREE DOZEN GERMAN FATHERLANDS!
FOUNDATION OF A UNITARY GERMAN REPUBLIC!

<The German philistines who read these leaflets raged beyond measure
at such high treason, or shook their heads, doubting the sanity of
the writer. They would sooner believe that the sky would tumble
down than that the 'by the grace of God' Hohenzollerns would
cease to bless Germany with their reign. Their slender capacity
to think was completely turned off by the press. For years they
were deceived daily by the illusion of a final victory to be awaited.
As the believer in his religion, so they believed in the truthful-
ness of the newspapers.> The criminal police set their spies in motion
when these leaflets appeared. They knew that their distribution
emanated from the *spiritus rectus* of the Spartacus League, but were
credulous enough to see him also as the author of all the leaflets
and articles that originated from Rosa Luxemburg's pen. Only the
total stupidity of the police prevented them from detecting the
characteristic style of Rosa Luxemburg for all these years.

As Leo Jogiches had worked until now with extreme caution
and only a few proven comrades, the police searched for him in
vain. If suspects were arrested and brought to testify under duress,
they might give a description of the conspirator but nobody knew
his proper name or even his address. Even letters which were found
across the country on house searches did not put them on the track.
These were always produced in a completely different hand or machine,
and Leo Jogiches time and again changed his signature, from Gross
to Kraft, Krummbügel or something else.

The longer the war lasted, the more it diminished our ranks;
comrades who seemed suspect to the authorities were marched
off to the trenches, others who could be proved to have been involved in anti-war activity were sent to prison or penal servitude.
Frightened by these rigorous measures, and not brave enough to
adapt to them, many people refused this work. Many others withdrew,
tired of fighting, because everything seemed so useless, or because
they were not up to the exertions of this exhausting work. There
was no compensation whatsoever, everyone voluntarily gave their
time and money. <The corruption and betrayal of socialism could

only set in towards the end of the war, when well-paid jobs were handed out and firmly clung on to.>[14]

Due to the lack of assistance Leo Jogiches had given up his 'motor duty'. Now, as there was hardly anyone else to do this, he took paper or stencils on his own back and brought them to the illegal print shops, often also collecting the finished printed matter himself. The principle of holding political discussions only with a few comrades, who then informed confidential representatives in the factories, had to be relinquished. Leo Jogiches now frequently held information and instruction workshops for twenty or more workers.

I informed Rosa Luxemburg of the position in which our friend found himself. She begged him not to expose himself to the danger of arrest. She said that 'a movement which relies on two eyes' was no movement. If viable, it would break a path for itself even if he went to Switzerland, as she advised him to do. For it could only be a matter of time before the long arm of the police reached him. And then this political criminal would face penal servitude, perhaps even the death penalty, as an 'enemy alien'. In the end I discussed with Leo Jogiches, who did not want to hear about leaving for Switzerland, what I could do in case of his arrest. Apart from food, there would be books and papers and other things to provide. Everything taken to a prisoner required written permission from the responsible judge.

<Given the scarcity even of the most awful ersatz chemical foods, meals in the prisons were insufficient; even rotten food was given. Underclothing had to be provided. Permission to send books and newspapers had to be requested from the appropriate judge. Awaiting the prisoner was a small, cold cell with a bowl, a lead spoon, a water jug and a wash-basin. For sleeping, a plank bedstead with bolster, a thin mattress and a woollen blanket. During the day the bedstead was placed upright and fixed to the wall. A wooden plank which served as table could also be tilted down. The only chair was firmly screwed down and in such a way that the prisoner had to face the door. The official who looked into the room from time to time could see what the prisoner was doing by means of a flap. Next to the door was the toilet, with automatic water flushing which operated for the whole prison in the morning, noon and evening. For every item that one wanted to bring the prisoner, one had to show the prison authorities the permission of the appropriate judge.> When someone was arrested, therefore, there were many things to be done before the prisoner could be provided with the most essential things. I myself would not be able to visit Leo

Jogiches in prison, nor to call on his judge. My connection with
Rosa Luxemburg would immediately have put the court on the
right track.

Leo Jogiches had no relations, and so it would be necessary
to find a 'fiancée' for him. Such 'fiancées' had proved useful for
prisoners without a family. If the prisoner had no girlfriend, one
was invented. But it proved rather difficult to select from the comrades
who might be considered, one who could perform this service for
Leo Jogiches. Time and again, with wit and humour, Leo Jogiches
refused as politically compromising the woman proposed to him.
When he said goodbye to me on the day before his arrest, he went
to a conference in Neukölln, with some twenty comrades taking
part. 'If anything happens to me, then,' he said, 'get in touch with
my landlady, she will do everything necessary for me.' I was the
only person, apart from Franz Mehring, who knew the landlady's
address; I was not allowed to give it to anybody, not even the most
trusted.

On the days when Leo Jogiches did not come to me, he used
to telephone. He told me where he could be reached, as anybody
who wanted to speak to him turned to me. We had a rather com-
plicated way of understanding each other. No names were given,
everybody either had a nickname or was described in such a way
that anyone listening in on behalf of the authorities — which was
not infrequent — could not find out anything. How many hours
did I wait anxiously, when I expected Leo Jogiches at a certain time
and he did not come. He was certainly unpunctual; not seldom,
when he had arranged to be with me during the morning, he appeared only towards evening. I was glad that he came and generally did not reproach him.

But when on 10 March 1918 neither a telephone call came
nor Leo Jogiches himself, by late in the evening I knew that his
fate was sealed. The next morning I travelled to his flat. He had
been arrested there the previous morning, but a search of the flat
yielded no results. <As was usual, the prisoner was first of all taken
in police custody to Alexanderplatz. I asked the landlady to look
after Leo Jogiches. She willingly agreed and obtained everything
necessary, but she was jealous when now and then a woman ad-
mirer turned up at the prison. She then raged at Leo Jogiches and
afterwards complained to me. This landlady was an attractive woman,
still young, whose husband had been killed in action. Leo Jogiches
had remarked on occasion that she was morbidly curious. There
were no limits to what she would do in the way of prying into his
affairs. She even opened letters that came for him. When I visited

the landlady I introduced myself under a false name. She asked immediately if I was the wife of the man with the grey beard, which for the sake of simplicity I confirmed. She was thinking of Franz Mehring, the sole visitor that Leo Jogiches had had there. Leo Jogiches had generally phoned me from a tobacconist's near his flat. The landlady, whom the shopkeeper had informed of this, asked him to note the number he asked for. And since, when I answered the telephone, Leo Jogiches addressed me as Mathilde — or when I was not there asked my family for Mathilde — the woman was not content until she had discovered all my personal details. She told Leo Jogiches one day triumphantly that she knew whom he always telephoned. As I did typing work, he pretended that he was having a rather large job for a friend done by me, but from then on he preferred not to make telephone calls in his neighbourhood. Naturally the landlady knew nothing of Leo Jogiches's political interests or the people he had dealings with.>

The lady behaved very well. When she brought food and things to Leo Jogiches in the Alexanderplatz prison, the officer on duty said she should be ashamed at providing for a man who had tried to contaminate the brave German army with his leaflets; she should give the food to the poor people. 'The food belongs to Herr Jogiches,' replied the woman, 'and if the man is so despicable then Germans should not accept anything from him.' She prevailed, and Leo Jogiches now had the first sign that we knew where he was.

After a few days he was remanded to the Moabit prison. As I was unknown there at this time, I was able to negotiate with the officials and by signing the landlady's name on the register I could bring everything Leo Jogiches needed. As the landlady was professionally engaged during the day, while things for the prisoner could be brought only in the morning, she accepted my help. Despite strict supervision in the Moabit prison I could give Leo Jogiches the political news, and he always invented new ways of smuggling. 'All private things interest me too,' read a communication from the great Leo that I deciphered in the first few days, although he had given me strict orders never to add private stories or expressions of sentiment in reports to Rosa Luxemburg — 'Such rubbish is not worth running risks for.'

The judge in charge of the examination, [Hugo] Holthöfer, was delighted to have the traitor Jogiches under lock and key. For several months he had been sought, and it had been very hard for the police to catch him. Leo Jogiches had figured largely in a high treason trial against Bertha Thalheimer,[15] who after six months on remand was sentenced to two years' penal servitude; she did not serve the whole of this in Delitzsch, as the November revolution set her free. This comrade had come to Berlin from Stuttgart in order to support Leo Jogiches in his political activity. She had rented a room in Südende. In the adjoining room, unknown to Bertha Thalheimer, lived an editor of the Scherl press,[16] who tried to listen to her talks with Leo Jogiches. Bertha Thalheimer's sister-in-law was also involved in the case because she had written in longhand a duplicating stencil with an appeal, which was a punishable offence.

During the trial the landlady, the neighbouring tenant, the sister-in-law and many others were called as witnesses. Some could not give a correct description of Leo Jogiches, others would not. Furthermore, neither the landlady nor the neighbour could give any positive evidence. The party comrades involved in the process, besides, blamed everything on the legendary individual who played a role in the police spies' report, in the belief that this 'clever fox' could not be caught by the 'bloody' police — as Leo Jogiches used to express himself. They considered themselves safe because the personal description was incorrect and they assumed that the police spies would not find Leo Jogiches. But now the fox was in the trap, to the delight of the presiding judge — who looked forward to material for the Thalheimer trial — and to the horror of his friends.

Leo Jogiches did not make it easy for this gentleman, who was also the prosecutor in his case. At the hearing he refused to talk, so that the judge had to hold a monologue. Leo Jogiches disguised his handwriting, and no graphologist could detect that it was the same handwriting that was known from the conspirative letters ascribed to him. To the shame of some of the comrades arrested with him it must be said that they did not behave in prison like revolutionaries. Softened up, they allowed themselves to give evidence. In spite of this, due to his skilful conduct no punishable action could be proved on Leo Jogiches.

Before the case was transferred to judge Holthöfer I had to show the investigating magistrate the food which I brought to the prison. This official generally returned me part of the food. Did I imagine that traitors came into prison to enjoy food and drink? A starvation diet was more appropriate for such people. All books had likewise to be shown to the official. Authors like John Galsworthy, Knut Hamsun, even Leo Tolstoy were unknown to him. 'What are you thinking of,' he shouted. 'No one has heard of such authors. I don't know what is in the books, the titles are harmless enough but that does not mean anything. Bring classics or books from Engelhorn's fiction library, then I know they are good books which I can permit to be read.' As soon as Holthöfer became legally responsible for the case I was allowed to bring food every ten days, later weekly, but nothing cooked. We soon found out that the officials responsible for taking the food could be bribed. Only a small amount of food was allowed to be handed in, but for a small tip the officials' hearts softened and our prisoners did not have to go hungry.

After I had undertaken everything necessary for Leo Jogiches I travelled to Rosa Luxemburg, who expected me impatiently. Much as she had trembled for Leo Jogiches during his illegal activity, she calmly accepted the irrevocable. She forbade any food being brought for her. She was well nourished in Breslau and I had to care now for Leo Jogiches. 'You know that the prison food is inedible and Leo lives almost entirely on what you bring him. Please tell me what that is.' I gave her a list. 'I can see you're managing things well. I would not have expected anything less from you.' <I had to 'manage things well' for all of seven months.> On every visit Rosa Luxemburg gave me some little morsel for Leo Jogiches, which she either had saved herself or had Frau Schlisch obtain in Breslau. She also took care of cigarettes, as Leo Jogiches was a smoker. It was quite in keeping with Rosa Luxemburg's way that she suggested to me having her sheets cut up in case Leo Jogiches was short of underclothes, which however was not the case.

What mattered now was not to interrupt the appearance of the *Spartakus-Briefe* [Spartacus letters]. Apart from leaflets, this was the only organ through which the Spartacus Group could speak to the masses. The continuing appearance of this paper, moreover, would divert suspicion from the prisoner. Leo Jogiches recommended letting Wolfgang Fernbach[17] edit the paper, a young and very gifted friend of ours who had worked with great selflessness during the war. Leo Jogiches would himself make the precise choice of articles and their arrangement. I informed Ernst Meyer, who had been released from prison in the meantime, of this decision. Ernst Meyer suffered from a lung disease. His physical strength could not withstand the constant strain of illegal work, and in desperation at the attitude of the German proletariat he had withdrawn from this. After Leo Jogiches's arrest, however, he made himself available and again took on the publication of the *Spartakus-Briefe*.

5. Revolution and Tragedy

In March 1918, some six months after the seizure of power by the Bolsheviks in Russia, the people's delegates from the Russian Federal Soviet Republics[66] came as diplomatic representatives to Berlin and immediately sought to make contact with the opposition German Social-Democrats. Now even the most cowardly saw fit to set to work once more, from a sense of shame towards the Russians. The delegates sent to the Berlin embassy were no mental giants, but they inspired readiness for sacrifice and devotion to the revolution. I occasionally went to them to report on Rosa Luxemburg and Leo Jogiches. They spoke with glowing eyes of these two revolutionaries and offered to make financial contributions for the pair. I declined this, as neither Rosa Luxemburg nor Leo Jogiches would have accepted it. <It was touching with what love a considerable number of parcels had been packed which Russians freed from prison by the revolution sent their German brethren still in captivity, among whom of course Rosa Luxemburg and Leo Jogiches were not forgotten.>

A feverish co-operation between Russian and German comrades now commenced. Besides the old stock of revolutionary Social-Democrats others now flocked in, attracted partly by the large salaries which the Russians paid and partly by the position of power. I remember party comrades, close friends of the Mensheviks, who suddenly took positions in the Russian embassy. They had 'convinced' themselves that they had misjudged the Bolsheviks and were now pioneers of Bolshevism in Germany.

Out of deep conviction to serve the Russian revolution, Paul Levi came to Berlin in summer 1918. He had spent a considerable part of the war convalescing in Switzerland, and made connections there with Lenin and Radek. Happy that Lenin had managed to convert his plans into deeds, Paul Levi did not now intend to resume his civilian profession as lawyer. He instead did everything in his power for the revolution in Germany that the Spartacists hoped for, whose outbreak leaders of the USPD considered a misfortune even on the eve of the overthrow.

At the end of August and the beginning of September 1918 I

made my last prison visits to Rosa Luxemburg. We had agreed that
I should choose a place for my autumn holiday that made it possible to stop in Breslau on my journey there and back. Rosa Luxemburg
made efforts to find a suitable resort, and heard from the prison
warders that they liked to go for their leave to the Glatzer mountains which had beautiful scenery and were within easy reach of
Breslau. For the first visit I had thought of a little deception. Without
going first to the *Kommandantur* I went to the prison and told
the warder on duty that I wanted to discuss with Frau Luxemburg
when she wanted to have outings and visitors. The warder brought
the prisoner down into the yard and Rosa Luxemburg embraced
me fiercely. She had just been in a depressed mood, from which
this surprise freed her. How great was her joy when in one of the
papers I left in her cell she found an article by Leon Trotsky that
had just been published in Germany, 'From the October Revolution to Brest-Litovsk'. <I had placed it in a harmless newspapaper
and on leaving I asked for permission to leave this with Rosa
Luxemburg, which the supervisor gave.>

After some excursions with the prisoner, I travelled to the
mountains alone. Since I frequently passed on letters from Paul
Levi, or transmitted his reports to Rosa Luxemburg in coded message, this was a necessary precaution. <Ever since my thoughts
had been almost exclusively with Rosa Luxemburg, I had been
accustomed to travel alone. As I wrote her secret letters almost
daily, to be alone was also a necessary precaution. Ambling through
the countryside, I was never free of the painful feeling of Rosa
Luxemburg's confinement in prison; then it made me happy to
send her flowers and tell her about my walks, and in this way bring
variety into her monotonous life. At the same time we both keenly
looked forward to my return journey via Breslau.>

As arranged I visited Rosa Luxemburg again in prison on my
return journey. From a window I saw her walking to and fro in
the 'kitchen garden'. After I had drawn her attention to me I called
down: 'Have you read today's paper?' 'Yes,' she shouted, understanding what my question meant. The papers announced the impending military collapse of Austria, after which the defeat of Germany
had to follow. <The papers announced Bulgaria's withdrawal from
the war, a sign of Germany's impending catastrophe. This was the
first lightning on the political horizon, soon to be followed by the
most tremendous thunderclaps. After we'd had to see the German
working class celebrate 'victories' for four whole years, and anyone who held that victory or defeat meant the same for them was
considered a fool, many could easily lose courage. Rosa Luxemburg

however never lost courage. When we begged her in October 1917 to take serious steps to go to Russia, she replied: 'I am too bound up with the shame of the German working class; I will not capitulate.' When we later on repeated our request she replied: 'No, I remain at my post, and I still hope to experience something in Germany, and in the not too distant future at that.' At the end of September we made our last Breslau excursion by car. 'Rosa,' I said suddenly, 'when you're released from prison, give away all your things here.' 'Do you really think we shall also have a revolution here?' asked the lawyer accompanying us. 'Yes,' said Rosa Luxemburg, 'I really believe it now. You see, if Bulgaria gives up the struggle, Turkey will soon be forced to ask for a separate peace, which would mean Hungary and Austria having to drop out soon after. That leaves Germany alone on the battlefield, and under these circumstances it cannot hold out alone. Whether this happens very soon, or the catastrophe will drag out, I cannot judge. But Germany's fate is sealed.' The lawyer thought that if Germany gathered all its force it would manage to carry the battle to victory even alone. But hardly two months after this conversation we experienced the collapse of Germany and its allies.>

The dungeons of the political martyrs opened. A few weeks before the state was overthrown, the German government announced an 'amnesty'. A mere gesture, as the revolution was already impending and the storming of the prisons was bound to follow. Karl Liebknecht was among those reprieved. He was released from penal servitude on 23 October. An impatient crowd awaited him on the platform and around [Berlin's] Anhalt station. As the train was unexpectedly late the fear arose that it had been diverted by order of the government to avoid an undesirable reception and demonstration. When the train finally arrived the waiting crowd gave vent to an outburst of joy. Soldiers in grey lifted their beloved leader on their shoulders and carried him onto an open lorry that was waiting. Karl Liebknecht, his fists clenched, called repeatedly: 'Down with the government! Down with the war!', the same words for which he had been imprisoned and which he had called out in court after his conviction. The jubilation of the masses was so spontaneous and overpowering that the police could not immediately control the situation. But eventually they gained the upper hand and barred the streets around Anhalt station by a closed chain of policemen, preventing the masses from following Liebknecht's car which was driven to the Russian embassy.

    <On the following evening, the Russians gave a small dinner

to honour Karl Liebknecht. We ate from the former tsars' table service. The Russian tsars' coat-of-arms on the dishes, the silverware and the crystal goblets signalled proverbially the perishability of all things. My mood was disturbed by the thought that Rosa Luxemburg would not have approved of such a meal at a time when the ordinary people were suffering from hunger. Most of the speeches, too, which almost all dwelt on the expected revolution, were meaningless, and did not do justice to the conditions of the time. As Hugo Haase left the embassy, when the Russians once again expressed their hope for the coming overthrow in Germany, he said that a revolution would have to be considered a misfortune.> A few days later the Russian diplomatic mission was expelled by the Prussian government.

A shorthand note of Paul Levi from those days, which he dictated to me for secret transmission to Rosa Luxemburg, escaped destruction. This note gives an insight into the activity of the revolutionary workers shortly before the outbreak of the revolution, so I am quoting it verbatim:

> Firstly your case. I do not expect particular success from the military authorities. I want to undertake these steps to avoid later on a 'negative conflict of responsibility' arising and the case being shifted from one party to another. Afterwards the Chancellor will say that if we had acted by the rules, the custody order would have been lifted, while the military authorities will say that if they had been given orders, the order would have been lifted. I want to prevent these silly excuses. They should now admit the custody order publicly in all form and in reasoned manner. Apart from this I shall try as soon as I am again in Berlin to call on Gröber[2] who is the Chancellor's deputy in matters concerning the state of siege, on the assumption that Haase has not yet done anything. If he had already taken steps in this direction mine would be unnecessary. Further personal matters: Karl [Liebknecht] and Erna [Ernst Meyer] strongly want me to remain here and and I expect to move here permanently at the end of this week.
>
> Here then is some news in no particular order, simply in the sequence I have noted things:
>
> 1) Significant as a sign of the atmosphere in the army divisions is the following information: On Friday the fleet was supposed to strike a great blow against England. The fleet sailed out, but returned after a while without having carried out its objective as the whole fleet mutinied. It is said that the Scheidemanns had already taken the matter in hand and tried to throttle it. I do not know any more details myself. The atmosphere in the army is supposed to be marvellous. Lekk. [Karl

Liebknecht] told me early this morning as an example that in the individual guards regiments crack battalions had been formed from which all Berliners and in fact everyone from the large cities were excluded. According to Lekk's informants the atmosphere is such that it is impossible that even these crack battalions would shoot at the people. Probably there will be fraternisation.

Less happy is the position among the workers, or among those that call themselves the workers' representatives. On Saturday evening the Workers' Council was in session and defeated by 23 votes to 19 the action and demonstration planned for Monday.[3] The decision had a terribly depressing effect on our people. As at present we lack any mechanism to mobilise the masses independently, we decided on Sunday to push for a transformation of the Workers' Council, given that at present this Workers' Council consists essentially of the dissatisfied opposition of the Metal Workers' Union and nobody else. The friends who know the movement here better maintain that this would offer some prospects. Yesterday Lekk. was all day with confidantes at long conferences in the Trade Union House, and depressed as he had been yesterday, today he arrived equally hopeful. The atmosphere has completely changed and the people are ready. The Workers' [Council] executive, which is, I believe, if I have understood correctly, the immediate extension of the Workers' Council, is in permanent session, so that decisions can be made at any time, and on Wednesday all shop stewards are to assemble and will possibly pass new resolutions. From my experience the atmosphere is brilliant. I was recently in meetings in South Germany where the mood was excellent though the speaker Vogtherr deserved to be hung by the legs.[4] Now he is peddling Wilson as he previously did Marx and KK [Karl Kautsky]. You will have read in the *Vossische [Zeitung]* of the latest demonstrations in Stuttgart.[5] What appears to me most valuable about these demonstrations is that they seem to have taken place quite spontaneously. For on Thursday I was still in Stuttgart and there was no sign of it and not even anything planned. The Daimler works are said to be completely in our hands, and according to the latest news it does not seem to be different at Bosch.

Further. We are to get here in Berlin in the next few days a daily newspaper with 34,000 subscribers, and indeed ourselves and not the USP [Independents]. How the question of editor is to be solved is still outstanding, we will try to get Thalheimer[6] for it. The Stuttgart paper will be expanded at the same time. It appears twice weekly. Negotiations with Bremen for taking over the A.P. *[Arbeiter-Politik]* are still under way.[7] Our conditions are as you know, exclusion of Borchardt;[8] an editor to be be appointed by us; the press commission to comprise: 3 from Bremen, 3 from Berlin, 1 from Hamburg. It will be good if we get hold of the paper.

As I see it, the following points have to be considered in the immediate future, as the questions are now becoming acute: question of soviets or constituent assembly; question of dictatorship of the proletariat. The arming of the Berlin workers seems to be considerably more favourable lately. Weapons have been acquired, approx. 2500. *Order of the Day* no. 1 has appeared.[9] I have not seen it yet. The person officially responsible is [Wilhelm Pieck, as he lived there in Steglitz] and remains here now. In Duisburg arrests have occurred. I am going there on Thursday and will have a look round.

Leo Jogiches was not among those amnestied. On 8 November he was collected from prison by Paul Levi, who later describes the events as follows:[10]

[...] I went together with a friend [...] about two o'clock to the Moabit prison, where we knew our friend was still held, Leo Jogiches who was later murdered. No great legitimation was necessary. Some commotion, the door opened and the warder asked what we wanted. 'Bring out the political prisoners.' 'There are none here.' 'Yes, at least Leo Jogiches.' 'One moment, the governor will come immediately.' And he came. He was very small; he said he had only the one, Leo Jogiches, the others had all left; we should not make such a noise and disturb the criminal prisoners. We said that we had to fetch Leo Jogiches right away ourselves; so we went, followed by the governor and two guards, just the two of us, through the large prison until we reached the sick bay where he was lying. They could of course have locked us up while we were there. But at that time the royal Prussian officials were still well-behaved; they gave us our friend and the three of us marched happily off. [...]

I also saw Leo Jogiches in the course of this day. Owing to an attack of flu which he had not yet overcome he was so weak that he found walking difficult. Now we had to get Rosa Luxemburg, who also had not been amnestied. On the morning of 9 November, the day the revolution broke out, Rosa Luxemburg phoned me from Breslau. She had been informed at 10 p.m. on 8 November by the Breslau prison directorate that she was free. But as she had not packed all her things, and moreover did not want to go to the Schlisch family at such a late hour, she remained that night in the prison. Train traffic between Breslau and Berlin had been suspended for civilian travellers in the first days of the revolution due to troop transports, so that the impatiently expected — and herself quite impatient — Rosa Luxemburg could not start the journey home. She took part in the Breslau demonstrations which greeted the young republic. <In the evening she walked with party friends

through the streets of Breslau, where the revolution had been proclaimed.>

Leo Jogiches decided that on 10 November, if I still could not use the train, I should fetch Rosa Luxemburg by car. Then she let me know by telephone that the trains were now going as far as Frankfurt-an-der-Oder and that we should fetch her from there. Leo Jogiches wanted to travel together with me to meet his friend. She was immediately to accompany him to the assembly of the Workers' and Soldiers' Councils in the Busch Circus. On 10 November a car collected me, but instead of Leo Jogiches the art historian Eduard Fuchs arrived, who explained that our friend was unavoidably detained. Fuchs wished very much to speak with Rosa Luxemburg immediately; he said she was wrongly informed about Russia. Despite many attempts by him and other comrades, Rosa Luxemburg had not given up her critical opinion of the Bolsheviks' tactics. *

But Eduard Fuchs did not manage to have the discussion he wanted that day. For the car, an open truck which apart from the escort had room for only two persons, broke down at the very start of the journey. Twice Fuchs requisitioned other cars at army depots, which proved even less serviceable, so that we failed to get to Frankfurt.

During the journey I observed the public in Berlin and in the suburbs. They were silent and showed no enthusiasm, apart from the occasional pedestrian who waved at our car bedecked with red flags. None of the soldiers in the fifteen or so men escorting us knew Rosa Luxemburg. When through the journey together we got into conversation, I was asked with some embarrassment who actually was this Rosa Luxemburg that we wanted to fetch. We travelled for five hours in unsuitable vehicles, and finally reached a station in the Berlin suburbs. Here we left the truck and our escort to their fate, and returned to the city by train.

In the meantime Rosa Luxemburg had arrived in Berlin. She had undertaken the journey in an overcrowded train, sitting on a

---

* See *Spartakus-Briefe* (new edition), Verlag A. Seehof & Co., Berlin; 'Die russische Tragödie', p.181. An expanded critique, which was likewise intended for the *Spartakus-Briefe,*was not published due to the outbreak of revolution in the meantime, and has been lost. As a number of copies existed, it is hoped that the presentation will still be found. Rosa Luxemburg, *Die russische Revolution, eine kritische Würdigung. Aus dem Nachlass von Rosa Luxemburg, herausgegeben und eingeleitet von Paul Levi.* Verlag Gesellschaft und Erziehung GmbH, Fichtenau-Berlin 1922.

suitcase in the corridor hemmed in between luggage and passengers. When it became known on the way that the train was going all the way to Berlin, and Rosa Luxemburg did not see any of her friends at Frankfurt, she remained sitting on her suitcase. The train came into Schlesischer station and Rosa Luxemburg stood a little while in confusion with her luggage, until she had the idea of phoning my mother.[11] She advised her to come to her as it was certain that I would get in touch with her. And this I did very soon after.

I then went immediately with Rosa Luxemburg to the editorial office of the *Berliner Lokal-Anzeiger* which on 9 November had been requisitioned by some romantic revolutionaries. An evening paper with the title *Die Rote Fahne* [Red Flag] was published with the technical staff of the Scherl company, followed by a morning edition for the next day, then the *Lokal-Anzeiger* was back again under its old regime. Leo Jogiches led Paul Levi, Karl Liebknecht, Ernst Meyer and Rosa Luxemburg from the Scherl offices to the Hotel Excelsior opposite the Anhalt station. It was agreed that for the time being they would not go home but stay in the Hotel Excelsior to be able to readily confer with each other. Paul Levi has described the publication of the *Rote Fahne* at the Scherl company, and the rapid end of this episode, appropriately and in due perspective in the feature from the Zwickau *Volksblatt-Almanach* already mentioned:[12]

> One of our friends had picked up ten soldiers somewhere on the street, and impelled to heroic deeds — 'a lieutenant and ten men' — he occupied the *Berliner Lokal-Anzeiger.* [...] This was on the Sunday. [...] This conquest of ours seemed secured by those ten men, who stood at the door armed to the teeth and let no one through unless they at least maintained they were with us. On Monday morning [the 11th] we came back. [...] We were all gathered — Rosa Luxemburg, Karl Liebknecht, ten or twelve other comrades — when suddenly the door opened, the publishing director appeared and declared that there would be no further edition. That's a bit cheeky, we thought. [...] When one of us tried to leave in order to go to the Workers' and Soldiers' Council, he found rifles pointed at him at the door of the building. The Scherl company had bought over our guard, who now declared that none of us would leave the building alive unless the company agreed. [...] And so we sat, a dozen prisoners of our own military force, on the third day of the revolution, and wondered how a revolution was to proceed if the 'revolutionary soldiers' could be so speedily snapped up by any capitalist at will between first and second breakfast.
>
> That was only an episode. But there is no episode that does not contain a part of the whole event. It was almost a symbol of the revolution.

Rosa Luxemburg's luggage was still at the Schlesischer station. I was told it was useless for me to go there, as I had no permit. It was essential in those days to have this if you wanted to go out on the streets at night. I was firmly resolved to try my luck even without a permit and in fact I was allowed to pass everywhere as soon as I said I had to collect Rosa Luxemburg's suitcase. When I brought the luggage to the hotel, late in the evening, our friends were still sitting together in political discussions. When everybody else agreed, Karl Liebknecht would still have a different opinion on one point or another. He could discuss for hours about some detail in order to prevail. This evening he was quiet and a little depressed! Leo Jogiches had only been able to restrain him with some effort from joining the coalition government with Haase and Ledebour. <He was ashamed now of his intention and so decisions were reached relatively quickly. Around midnight all separated and went to their rooms. I went for a moment to Leo Jogiches to give him a message. When I returned to Rosa Luxemburg's room, Karl Liebknecht was standing with her at the window and admiring the starry sky. The star of her misfortune was not yet visible that evening.>

The Spartacus leadership refused to make a pact with the bourgeoisie, as a fundamental principle was now involved. Rosa Luxemburg gave her reasons for this point of view in the Spartacus programme:

> With the outcome of the world war bourgeois class rule has forfeited its right to exist. It is no longer able to lead society out of the catastrophic economic collapse which the imperialist orgy has left behind. [...] The socialist revolution is the first which can attain victory only in the interest of the great majority and by the great majority of the workers [...] the economic transformation can take place only as a process carried by proletarian mass action. The naked decrees of the higher authorities of the revolution about socialisation are empty words. [...] It is not where the wage slave sits next to the capitalist, the rural proletarian next to the junker in a false equality to discuss in parliamentary style their questions of existence: but where the million-strong proletarian mass grasp the complete power of the state with their calloused hands, to dash their hammer like the god Thor on the head of the ruling class: there alone is a democracy which is not a deceit of the people...[..] In this final class struggle of world history, for the highest aims of humanity, the right word to the enemy is: thumb in the eye, knee on the chest.*

* *Was will der Spartakusbund?* First published in December 1918 in the *Rote Fahne*, then as a pamphlet. Later supplemented with an explanatory preface by Paul Levi, as this proved necessary.

During the first days of the revolution Rosa Luxemburg lived under constant harassment. Visitors arrived from far and near, and from all ranks of society, many of whom anticipated the Spartacists coming to power and scented advantages for themselves. Discussions took place on the political questions of the day, meetings were held and not last was the struggle for the ownership of the Scherl publishing house, which it was intended to buy. But the attempts to continue printing the *Rote Fahne* there failed. 'Oh,' said Rosa Luxemburg after the last hopeless efforts, 'the *Rote Fahne* will flutter over my grave!' Finally a successful agreement was reached with the *Kleiner Journal* in Königgrätzer Strasse. There the *Rote Fahne* was founded on 18 November with Karl Liebknecht and Rosa Luxemburg as responsible editors. With this Rosa Luxemburg took up her activity as editor-in-chief whilst Karl Liebknecht devoted himself mainly to agitation among the masses. He hardly permitted himself a few hours' sleep, spoke daily at three or four meetings, in factories and public places, and was everywhere that he was needed.

Most of the leading articles of this period were written by Rosa Luxemburg. Paul Levi also wrote valuable contributions to questions of the day and took some of the load off Rosa Luxemburg, as he was one of her closest collaborators. But neither he nor the other editorial staff were sufficiently conversant with newspaper publishing, and so Rosa Luxemburg hardly ever finished the necessary tasks before 11 p.m., and often only after midnight. She decided on the sequence of the articles, notices and news, she carried out a final proofing of the text before the paper went into press. If she did not take care of these things, something would go wrong, and she hated it that a paper which appeared under her name should contain errors. <She was awaiting Dr [Julian] Marchlewski (Karski), an experienced newspaperman, used to working together with Rosa Luxemburg. He arrived only after her death.>

A general hate campaign against the *Rote Fahne* and the Spartacists got under way. The Hotel Excelsior got rid of its Spartacist guests to show that it had nothing to do with them. Now they moved from one hotel to another and lived separately. Very soon these revolutionaries had to live under false names. The hotels around the Anhalt Station already knew the Spartacists looking for rooms and refused to have them stay. Tired of moving around, Rosa Luxemburg returned to her flat about the middle of December. I went with her. Between midnight and one o'clock I would fetch her from the train after making arrangements on the phone.

When she lay down in bed she stretched out contentedly like a
child and said: 'I shall sleep well. I've done everything that I wanted
to do. I am so happy.'

During the last days of December the Spartacus League became the Communist Party of Germany. At the founding congress,
the putschist tendency in the new party was frighteningly apparent.[13] Karl Liebknecht, Paul Levi, and not least Rosa Luxemburg,
tried in vain to combat it. As she said in her speech:[14]

> For us the conquest of power will not be effected at one blow. It will
> be a progressive act, for we shall progressively occupy all the
> positions of the capitalist state, defending tooth and nail each one
> that we seize. Moreover, in my view and in that of my most intimate
> associates in the party, the economic struggle, likewise, will be
> carried on by the workers' councils. The settlement of economic
> affairs, and the continued expansion of the area of this settlement,
> must be in the hands of the workers' councils. The councils must
> have all power in the state. To these ends must we direct our
> activities in the immediate future, and it is obvious that, if we pursue
> this line, there cannot fail to be an enormous and immediate
> intensification of the struggle. For step by step, by hand-to-hand
> fighting, in every province, in every town, in every village, in every
> commune, all the powers of the state have to be transferred bit by
> bit from the bourgeoisie to the workers' and soldiers' councils.
> But before these steps can be taken, the members of our own
> party and the proletarians in general must be schooled and
> disciplined. Even where workers' and soldiers' councils already exist,
> these councils are as yet far from understanding the purposes for
> which they exist. We must make the masses realise that the workers'
> and soldiers' council has to be the central feature of the machinery
> of state, that it must concentrate all power within itself, and must
> utilise all powers for the one great purpose of bringing about the
> socialist revolution. Those workers who are already organised to
> form workers' and soldiers' councils are still very far from having
> adopted such an outlook, and only isolated proletarian minorities
> are as yet clear as to the tasks that devolve upon them. But there is
> no reason to complain of this, for it is a normal state of affairs. The
> masses must learn how to use power, by using power. There is no
> other way. [...] Thus only can we mine the ground so effectively as
> to make everything ready for the revolution which will crown our
> work. Quite deliberately, and with a clear sense of the significance
> of our words, did some of us say to you yesterday, did I in particular
> say to you, 'Do not imagine that you are going to have an easy time
> in the future!' [...] History is not going to make our revolution an
> easy matter like the bourgeois revolutions. In those revolutions it
> sufficed to overthrow the official power at the centre, and to replace
> a dozen or so persons in authority. But we have to work from beneath.
> Therein is displayed the mass character of our revolution, one which

aims at transforming the whole structure of society. It is thus characteristic of the modern proletarian revolution, that we must effect the conquest of political power, not from above, but from beneath.

The ninth of November was an attempt, a weakly, half-hearted, half-conscious, and chaotic attempt, to overthrow the existing public authority and to put an end to ownership rule. What is now incumbent upon us is that we should deliberately concentrate all the forces of the proletariat for an attack upon the very foundations of capitalist society. There, at the root, where the individual employer confronts his wage slaves; at the root, where all the executive organs of ownership rule confront the objects of this rule, confront the masses; there, step by step, we must seize the means of power from the rulers, must take them into our own hands. Working by such methods, it may seem that the process will be a rather more tedious one than we had imagined in our first enthusiasm. It is well, I think, that we should be perfectly clear as to all the difficulties and complications in the way of revolution. For I hope that, as in my own case, so in yours also, the description of the great difficulties we have to encounter, of the augmenting tasks we have to undertake, will neither abate zeal nor paralyse energy. [...] The greater the task, the more fervently will you gather up your forces. Nor must we forget that the revolution is able to do its work with extraordinary speed. I shall make no attempt to foretell how much time will be required. Who among us cares about the time, so long only as our lives suffice to bring it to pass? Enough for us to know clearly the work we have to do; and to the best of my ability I have endeavored to sketch, in broad outline, the work that lies before us.*

Rosa Luxemburg's warning voice was raised in vain.

At the first discussion about the posts to be allocated in the new party, Rosa Luxemburg had asked for me as her secretary. Unfortunately at this time I did not always show her the necessary understanding. Thousands of details pulled me one way and another. Demands were made on Rosa Luxemburg far above her strength. She was accustomed to write everything by hand, so that I hardly came to work with her. There was no time left for mutual understanding. Instead of waiting patiently to see how things would develop, I worked with Leo Jogiches. 'I am pleased at your good taste,' Rosa Luxemburg said, 'but I cannot understand that you find Leo more patient than I am. He is the most difficult character

* Rosa Luxemburg, *Speech on the Programme. Given at the Founding Conference of the Communist Party of Germany (Spartacus League), 29-31 December 1918, Berlin.* Verlag Rote Fahne, Berlin 1919.

I know, whereas people manage to put up with me.' <At that time unfortunately, I could not.>

One evening I waited a long time in Südende for Rosa Luxemburg's telephone call, until Paul Levi informed me I should come to the editorial offices, it was not advisable for Rosa Luxemburg to go home. With the prevailing pogrom atmosphere it was uncertain if she would be safe in her flat. I arrived at Potsdamer Platz after long delay and ran to the editorial office, where Rosa Luxemburg was already waiting outside with Paul Levi. 'But how can you run like that!' Rosa Luxemburg said. Paul Levi accompanied us to a taxi and we went to my flat. Rosa Luxemburg leaned against me and said once again that I should have gone slower. 'I am so hungry,' she added, 'give me some of what you brought with you. Leo would say one should control oneself, but I must eat something.' <We enjoyed a few pieces of roast turkey which we had been given by a good friend. 'Rosa,' I said, 'I am afraid for you. What is going to happen?' 'If it threatens to get dangerous, we'll go away together in the next few days.'

Of course, nothing came of this. On the contrary, Rosa Luxemburg took in a young girl who had written to ask her for shelter after the death of Hans Diefenbach.[15] We had discussed together the young girl's coming, and I was completely in agreement with it. But when she arrived I left the flat. From now on I could not bring myself to visit Rosa Luxemburg. When I occasionally did so, I experienced such torture that I decided to stop my visits. Rosa did not understand anything of this. 'I can't understand why you don't come to see me,' she said on several occasions. 'It's not possible,' I replied. 'I work till late in the evening with Leo.' Indeed we worked from nine in the morning until twelve at night. If I was finished sooner, I hurried to the *Rote Fahne* office and accompanied Rosa Luxemburg from there to the station, but in spite of being asked every time I did not go to Südende. Once we walked to the station shortly before midnight, and Rosa Luxemburg was so tired that she could hardly talk. She said, 'Can you tell me why I live constantly like this, without any inclination to do so? I would like to paint and live on a little plot of land where I can feed and love the animals. I would like to study natural science but above all else to live peacefully and on my own, not in this eternal whirlwind.' I relayed this to Leo Jogiches. 'Don't worry about it, Mathilde. If Rosa lived differently she would be even less satisfied. She *cannot* live differently.'>

On 29 December Rosa Luxemburg phoned me. She had a few hours free, would I visit her. I replied that I couldn't come; then she said she would come to me. But in the event she had no spare time and later on she told me everything that had burst upon her. On one of the following days I went to the *Rote Fahne* offices. 'Are you finally coming to have a chat? How could you stay away so long; don't you see how I live?' But already Karl Liebknecht called from the adjoining room: 'Please, Rosa, come immediately to the meeting. We are waiting for you.' <We said a hasty goodbye. I went home with the best intentions for improving my relations with Rosa Luxemburg. Unfortunately these intentions could no longer be realised.>

The pogrom mood generated by the counter-revolution in the Berlin population became more threatening day by day. Rosa Luxemburg and Karl Liebknecht were taken to the home of the physician Dr Bernstein, the well-known anarchist and strike propagandist.[16] When I went to see them there, they had already moved to a worker's family in Neukölln. The doctor's family had feared that the safety of their persecuted guests would be endangered by the talk of the housemaid. As I was getting ready to leave for Neukölln the telephone rang. A comrade and friend agitatedly announced that Wolfgang Fernbach had been shot. I asked for the message to be repeated, I found it unbelievable. The previous day[17] I had spoken with our friend at the *Rote Fahne* office. He was full of confidence and had asked Leo Jogiches what he could do in the service of the revolution. 'Do you want to stand in for Eugen Leviné[18] as editor of the *Vorwärts*?' Leo Jogiches asked somewhat hesitatingly, on account of the danger involved: 'There is no editor there.' To the dismay of Rosa Luxemburg, the *Vorwärts* had been occupied by the Spartacists. 'Of course,' came the reply. Wolfgang Fernbach did not approach death unawares. With a firm hand he had written on an envelope after giving his address: '[...] I beg the finder in case anything happens to me and I am found helpless, severely wounded or dead, to send off the enclosed postcard immediately, if possible with a short note about the exact circumstances. In any case the sender should state the place where I was found...' He was a victim of the *Vorwärts* occupation. His wife herself found these lines on the body of her husband.

On the way to Neukölln I heard excited conversations: 'She should be cut to pieces and given to wild beasts.' The boundless incitement against Rosa Luxemburg and Karl Liebknecht was uttered in such bestial threats. When I reached my destination after making a detour, and was certain there were no informers behind me, I climbed four flights of stairs from a small courtyard to the pair's hiding place. I had the feeling, after talking to Rosa Luxemburg and her new host, that I should remain there to warn and help in time. 'But where will you sleep?' Rosa Luxemburg asked when I mentioned this wish, 'the comrade sleeps in the bed with her child and I myself lie on the couch.' It was a narrow, hard resting place. 'Oh,' intervened the comrade, 'it is alright for you to stay here as long as not so many people come. I am afraid that Karl and Rosa will be discovered here.' I thought it over. In the second room Karl Liebknecht was debating with a sizeable number of comrades. It was an awful muddle in the small room. 'Karl,' I begged. 'Let Rosa live on her own. The two of you shouldn't stay together, it's enough if one is discovered.' 'That is out of the question,' was the determined reply. 'We must stay together so as to be ready to consult with each other at any time.' All arguments against this were useless. 'Please,'' I said, 'come to Rosa for a moment.' Here I repeated my request that they should separate and added the news of Wolfgang Fernbach's death. 'That is impossible,' Karl Liebknecht exclaimed., 'you must be mistaken.' 'No, Karl, I am not mistaken, I have spoken with his family, it is true.' Rosa Luxemburg cried silently: 'I'll give you a letter, Mathilde, you must take it to Frau Fernbach tomorrow.' 'I'll write too,' said Karl Liebknecht, and expressed his sympathy in a few lines. Rosa Luxemburg's letter went something like this:

> Dear Comrade [Alice] Fernbach,
> I press your hand in your sorrow. I have already seen so many of my friends fall left and right of me. This is the fate of the revolutionary fighter. I myself have only the one wish, also to find death in the struggle for our ideal. I am convinced that you will be brave.

After Karl Liebknecht had returned to the comrades, Rosa Luxemburg told me that I would likely not find her in the flat the following evening, the lady was afraid to keep her there. Nearly everybody was afraid and it was difficult to find shelter for Rosa Luxemburg and Karl Liebknecht. I talked to the lady but she said she could no longer take the responsibility. People were coming nonstop; I should ask myself whether this would not attract attention in a back courtyard where she rarely had visitors. I could only agree with her, and I assured her we would try to find another lodging.

<'Oh, Mathilde,' said Rosa Luxemburg when I was again with her, 'I wish I were back in jail.' 'How can you wish something so terrible!' 'A thousand times better than running about like a vagabond. In prison I had my peace, there was my cell and nobody else had any business there. But here so many people come that I simply cannot bear it. Can you tell me for example what business Fräulein

J... has here? Yesterday when she came I ran away and sat with a book in the little bedroom. After she finally left I joined the comrades and heard from them in conversation that Leo was said to have been arrested. Imagine what a fright I got. You must search for him tomorrow and do everything possible.' I obviously wanted to do this, but had no chance. On this evening, though, I was driven to admit the guilt I felt towards Rosa Luxemburg. 'I must tell you, Rosa,' I began, 'I cannot get any peace, I was always in the wrong when I felt offended by you. I must ask you to forgive me and I promise to come in future when you call me. It is madness to want to claim you for myself.' 'But Mathilde, don't you understand that I took in the young girl out of piety towards our friend Hans Diefenbach, my relation with her is a completely different one.' 'No matter, Rosa, I regret my conduct and I have to tell you this.' Rosa Luxemburg laughed. 'You know, when Hans Diefenbach died I regretted not having told him various things. Say what you want, then you'll have nothing to regret after my death.' At that moment Karl Liebknecht arrived with the landlady and her little daughter. 'I propose we read something,' he said. 'Oh yes,' I interrupted, thinking this would please Rosa Luxemburg. She gave me a searching look, as I had not let her reply. And so we read, i.e. Karl Liebknecht read to us. First of all he read a fairy tale by Tolstoy, then something of Goethe. When saying goodbye — it was the last time I saw Rosa Luxemburg — I kissed her hand. As usual she pulled it away, embraced me and kissed me heartily on the mouth. Though Karl Liebknecht and the landlady were present I embraced Rosa Luxemburg and whispered that I would see her again the following day, that everything was in order now and I was happy.>

While we were talking, yet another comrade had arrived. He brought the news that Leo Jogiches had been arrested. Rosa Luxemburg was frightened and I promised to look after him. On saying goodbye she embraced and kissed me heartily.

*   *   *

The next morning, before finding out anything about Leo Jogiches or taking the letter to Frau Fernbach, I went to the *Rote Fahne*. There, at the instigation of the building manager, the government soldiers who had occupied the building took me to the Garde-Kavallerie-(Schützen)-Division barracks.[19] It sufficed that the manager had given the order: 'Arrest her, she also worked in the editorial office.'

It was some time before I was interrogated. Many comrades

as well as people not involved filled the room. Without being noticed, I was able to put the letters from Rosa Luxemburg and Karl Liebknecht into a sandwich which I intended to eat; but I was allowed to go to the toilet and, while accompanying soldiers with rifles at the ready waited outside the door, I tore up the letters and flushed them away. Had the letters been found on me they would have known that I was in contact with Rosa Luxemburg and Karl Liebknecht, on whose capture high rewards had been placed.

At the interrogation I was bodily searched. Some receipts were found, mainly for car journeys, and they assumed I must have done these journeys for the Communist Party. Though this did not justify an arrest I was taken to the Reichstag building where the 'Reichstag' regiment were wreaking havoc. Things here looked devastated. Nearly all the easy chairs and carpets had been deliberately slashed with knives, mirrors and windows demolished.

The troops encircled me like wild animals. They were in a frightening pogrom mood. Soldiers constantly came into the little room where I was at last locked up; they glared at me curiously, for on my arrival the news spread that it was Rosa Luxemburg who had been arrested. When I get out of here, I thought, I shall know how to protect Rosa Luxemburg from the threatening danger. Though I did get out, it was in company of brutalised soldiers who took me to my flat. Waiting there for me in my office sat Paul Levi. He had wanted me to write some letters for him, and we were taken together to the Moabit prison. Probably his arrest at that time saved his life; he often maintained this later on. For if he had been found with Rosa Luxemburg and Karl Liebknecht he would have been brutally killed just as they were. As I had not committed a 'punishable action' my lawyer was certain I would soon be released. I did not mind at all trying out the prison for myself, as I could now judge if I had provided adequately for my prisoners. I found that some details of my care could be faulted, and as I thought I had to reckon on Rosa Luxemburg's arrest I wanted to do some things better in future. After a few days a young lawyer deputising for Hugo Haase visited me. In reply to my question what was happening outside he replied: 'Nothing much, Rosa Luxemburg and Karl Liebknecht have been murdered. Now things are quiet again.' I stared at the bringer of this news, I could not hold back my tears and sobbed without stopping. <Then I went into my cell and plagued myself with guilt, thinking that my arrest had possibly caused Rosa's death.>

'When you are arrested it is almost always due to lack of precautions. Guard against this, or you will find yourself permanently in jail like several other comrades, which is no glory.' Rosa Luxemburg had given me this good advice at the beginning of the war. And now I had not been careful enough. I held it for certain that if I had not been imprisoned I would eventually have separated Rosa Luxemburg from Karl Liebknecht, and I suffered much from this fault. After one week[20] I was set free, as also was Paul Levi. <When we were outside the prison walls, he said: 'Do you know how I learned about it? I came into the prison office to collect my papers, and I read there the headlines in large letters that Karl and Rosa had been murdered. How frightful!' Leo Jogiches did not say a word when we saw each other again. I explained to him the reproaches which depressed me utterly; I told him of the misunderstandings which had occurred between Rosa and myself and he tried to free me of these. I am certain he was plagued by reproaches himself.>

One day after my release from prison, on 25 January, the burial of Karl Liebknecht and twenty-nine other victims of the January struggles took place at the Friedrichsfelde cemetery. <Wolfgang Fernbach was also among these. 'That Rosa had to atone so terribly for her weakness towards Karl,' I said to Leo Jogiches as we went together to the ceremony.> 'Karl and Rosa will also be together now in death,' said Leo Jogiches. 'Today we will bury an empty coffin to indicate symbolically the place where the mortal remains of Rosa will be placed in the soil. I hope that her little body will be found.' <The sight of the many open graves surrounded by lamenting relatives and friends was dreadful. We placed flowers on the empty coffin of Rosa Luxemburg. When her mutilated body, which barbarous soldiers had thrown in the Landwehr canal on the order of their officers, was laid to rest on 13 June, the coffin had already fallen to pieces and Leo Jogiches's grave was also in place.

After losing Rosa Luxemburg, I wanted to act towards Leo Jogiches in such a way that I would have nothing to regret in the event of his death. When on one occasion he was in a bad humour and unapproachable I said to him: 'You know I won't quarrel with you. I don't want to reproach myself again as with Rosa's death. Who knows what may still come in this terrible revolution.' 'As soon as orderly conditions are re-established,' he replied quietly, 'I will go to Scandinavia. That is where I want to live. It is the only country I have visited without Rosa. In other countries that I love and would like to return to, I would always be reminded of the time spent there with Rosa.'>

Rosa Luxemburg's funeral procession

6. Aftermath

As I feared for Leo Jogiches's life I begged him not to stay in his present flat. It was known to the police and it was all too easy to arrest him there. "You are right," he replied, "but I cannot leave my landlady now. Later it will be possible, but not at the moment. The woman deserves a certain gratitude for having cared for me during my time in prison, she would not understand if I left now." Evening after evening we left our workplace in the Wilhelmstrasse[1] together, and went to the Potsdam suburban station from where we had gone so often to Rosa Luxemburg. Leo Jogiches took the Circle line to Neukölln, while I took a tram. Sometimes I saw him suddenly reappear as he boarded the train and call out "Goodbye! I just wanted to see if you got on the tram." Our conversation always turned around Rosa Luxemburg. "Mathilde," he said, "I loved my mother dearly and I suffered for a long time when she was snatched from me by death at an early age. But I finally was reconciled with my fate. But I shall not get over the loss of Rosa." <During these busy days Leo Jogiches had no time left to mourn. As always, he was ready with a joke or an anecdote, an encouraging smile for his collaborators, and above all for the young people who loved him so. Hardly two months had passed, between work and the remembrance of our dead. March arrived which threatened to sweep away the revolution with its storms.>

In March we received news from a reliable source that our office was to be occupied by government troops. We therefore left the building, taking manuscripts and printed matter, and moved into illegal flats. At the removal Leo Jogiches was ever present, he took care that nothing was left which could have acquainted the counter-revolution with our work.

Early in March a general strike was proclaimed in Berlin by the oppositional workers. "The capitalists are shaking, the government is about to fall. Workers, proletarians, do not hesitate," was the wording of the Communist Party's appeal. The response of the reaction was to beat the strike bloodily down. We had to mourn many deaths, some assassinated, others fallen in street battles.

During these troubles the party congress of the Independent

Social-Democratic Party took place in Berlin. At this congress Clara
Zetkin left the USP and joined the Communist Party. Leo Jogiches
awaited her anxiously to discuss her sphere of work. <She wanted
to stay in Rosa Luxemburg's flat. Leo Jogiches refused to visit us
there. "I cannot do it," he said to me. "I can't understand how you
can." Half apologising, I added that I liked to go to Südende. But I
accompanied Leo Jogiches to the former Upper House in the
Leipzigerstrasse, where the USP party conference was taking place.>
"Please, Clara," I said conversationally while taking her from the
conference hall to Leo Jogiches, "Try to see that during the present
disorders Leo does not sleep at home, he has no right to expose
himself to such danger." I asked a young Polish comrade who I
knew was very devoted to Leo Jogiches to find some accommodation for him. "Will he follow the advice?" was the understandable reply. "He wants to stay at home," I confirmed. "Let us try. I
have a room with my brother in the Tiergarten quarter, there Leo
will be safe and well looked after. Please tell him that I expect him
at nine o'clock in the evening in front of the house." The young
Pole waited a long time in bad weather. Leo Jogiches did not come.
On the following day when the comrade had already spoken with
Leo Jogiches, he said to me laughingly: "You must not send someone
into the pouring rain if I have not agreed to come."

A few hours later, when I was with Clara Zetkin in the flat
in Südende, Leo Jogiches phoned us. He would like to come out
to us, did we had any food for him. We were surprised that contrary to his habits he wanted to come for a meal; we had plenty of
food and were pleased to spend the evening with him.[2] I met our
friend at the station, to lessen the pain of his return to the flat.
When we sat down, Leo Jogiches said, "It is beautiful here. I have
the feeling that Rosa might come any moment. We should keep
the flat, Mathilde, unless it is let already. Make a new contract
right away tomorrow."

Leo Jogiches could not have given me greater pleasure, and
Clara Zetkin was also quite content. "Now I only ask one thing
of you, Leo, even if you do not appreciate my persistence. Promise me not to stay at home any longer. It would be best if you could
go away for some time." "That is impossible. This is no time to
go on holiday." "You will have time when you sit in jail, and even
more if you are murdered." Leo Jogiches did not reply and we spoke
about other things. He left very late. When I took him to the station he begged me not to press him about the accommodation.
He had always acted in life on his own initiative and did not want
to change this.

The following day, it was Sunday, Clara Zetkin and I stayed on our own. The next day she left for Stuttgart and I accompanied her to the station. Actually on the way home I wanted to call at the Moabit criminal justice building to enquire after a comrade from the lawyers Theodor Liebknecht[3] and Kurt Rosenfeld.[4] But as I was very tired I postponed this to the following day. Early Tuesday morning I went to the Moabit to obtain a visiting permit for a woman comrade who was on remand. In one of the long corridors I met Kurt Rosenfeld. "Please come with me, I have something to tell you. Unfortunately nothing good," he added, after we entered one of the lawyers' rooms." "Leo has been arrested." "It's worse." "Have they killed him as well?" "It hasn't been confirmed. Read the notice here in today's *Vossische Zeitung*..." "Then there is no doubt!" "Newspaper reports aren't always correct, I have no real leads."

Kurt Rosenfeld left me and shortly afterwards Theodor Liebknecht entered. "What's the matter, Mathilde?" "Leo has been murdered." "But I know nothing about it." "Would you like to come with me to the morgue, Comrade Liebknecht? I want to be certain." We travelled to the morgue in Hannoverstrasse. "Shall I go in without you?" asked Theodor Liebknecht. "Stay outside, woman," the doorkeeper interjected, "you'll never get rid of the sight." Theodor Liebknecht went in on his own and returned soon. He had found the corpse of Leo Jogiches. "Frightening, so many dead!"

A witness who was also arrested on 10 March in Neukölln described the events of Leo Jogiches's murder in a newspaper article. I quote the report below:[5]

[...] In front of my house stood a huge lorry with armed soldiers accompanied by an armoured car. Some party comrades including Leo Jogiches were already standing on the lorry. [...] Our route led directly to the headquarters of the government troops, in the Berlin criminal justice building. After being handed over there we had first to wait for many hours in the corridor. Leo Jogiches was of the opinion that the "fun" would only last a few days. One might almost share his opinion, for suddenly we were taken to the remand prison which is in the same building. Unfortunately the director there did not want us. He explained energetically that everything was full up. So the guard who accompanied us returned to us with the remark: "What are we going to do with this rabble, the best is to shoot them down." Now the great puzzle, what to do with us, began. We were taken back to the first place, where we had to wait again. In the meantime the superior officers had also appeared. They enquired after us and occupied themselves in particular with Leo Jogiches. The infamous Tamschick appeared, and asked Leo Jogiches for his papers. He said he would show these at the proper time to the remand judge. Tamschik threatened him with a revolver and forced him to hand over his papers. A terrible ordeal began now for Leo Jogiches. We others were taken into a guardroom and once again searched for weapons. He was separated from us and had to stand close to a window. Later on he was called into the room of the officers where he was beaten mercilessly; one could hear outside how he was tortured, and then we saw him as he was pushed outside.

We others were led into a guard room and again searched for weapons. We were told that any attempt to escape would cost us our life. In any case an attempt to escape was hopeless with the rigid control of the entry and exit gates. We heard a revolver shot in the guard room which came from the floor of the criminal justice building. We had no further doubt that Leo Jogiches had become the victim of the enraged soldier Tamschik.[6] They had it in for Leo Jogiches, he was suspected of being the avenger of Rosa Luxemburg. It was he who had made public the information that explained the murders. He was feared, and was deliberately murdered. Despite this, after the murder of Leo Jogiches the false allegation was made to the public that he was "shot trying to escape".

I undertook the preparations for the funeral of Leo Jogiches, as all other comrades who might have been considered for this had to live in the strictest illegality. The trams did not run but there were cars and taxis. Together with Theodor Liebknecht I prepared in a few days everything necessary.

Käthe Kollwitz had drawn the dead Karl Liebknecht on his bier. I wished her artist's hand to preserve likewise for the future the death mask of Leo Jogiches. I wanted to ensure that she was at home before coming to request her agreement. Telephone connections were made only in urgent cases. As Käthe Kollwitz's husband was a well-known doctor I was allowed the call for a medical request. Instead I stated my wish, whereupon the telephone exchange broke the connection. Now I knew that I would find Käthe Kollwitz and I went to her at once. She received me kindly and said she was willing to do the drawing. In conversation she remarked that though she was not a member of the Communist Party, she had the strongest sympathy for its leaders who had lost their lives in such a dreadful fashion. I should also like to mention the answer Käthe Kollwitz gave when I asked her later on to set a fee: "Oh, I would not want to be paid for such a service." "May I beg that we refund the expenses for the car?" "I went from my house to the morgue on foot, I would not want to take a car at a time like this. I hope that my drawing was successful," and she showed two chalk drawings with a wonderfully preserved expression.

The funeral for Leo Jogiches at the Friedrichsfeld cemetery was simple and moving. The closest collaborators of the deceased stayed away, they could not expose themselves to the danger of arrest. The burial had not been officially advertised, yet a not inconsiderable number of party comrades who had honoured and loved the dead leader were present. The speeches given at his coffin were filled with genuine mourning and with the pledge to continue his uninterrupted struggle.

The March strike had not brought the desired success, on the contrary it had led to the retreat of the revolutionary movement. The Communist Party leaders, considered by the counter-revolution as fair game, were now forced to live underground and for security reasons moved to Frankfurt-am-Main. An illegal all-German conference was called there in order to re-establish the interrupted connections between the party leadership and the country. Publishing the *Rote Fahne* in Berlin had been made impossible by the state of siege. Printers could not be found nor was distribution possible. In order to provide Berlin with a replacement organ, Paul Levi and some other Berlin editors collaborated with the Hanau *Freiheit*. Hanau, close to Frankfurt, was a good revolutionary district, under the exemplary and clever leadership of the physician Dr Wagner.[7] The print run of the *Freiheit* was increased considerably and the copies required for Berlin were dispatched. But the distance was too great, they arrived too late at their destination, overtaken by events. So the base was changed again and moved to Leipzig, a city closer to Berlin. It was hoped to have the *Rote Fahne* fly in all directions once more from there.

After the murder of Leo Jogiches Paul Levi took on the leadership of the party. He frequently issued circulars with directives and reports on the political situation to accommodation addresses of the local Communist groups. Leipzig's central position also permitted personal contact with confidantes across the country. What aggravated matters however was that the political activists working in Leipzig were frequently required in Berlin. The rail connection was poor, trains went slowly and infrequently, so that travelling to Berlin took much time. Added to this was that not everybody worked with the same self-sacrificing courage. <Elements had crept in for whom the work was a way of earning money.> The more the Communist Party grew, the fewer in number were those really devoted. <Not a few comrades who during the war had been selfless and devoted to the cause had been corrupted by the high wages and the money readily earmarked for illegal purposes, the value of which they failed to understand.>

The appearance of the *Rote Fahne* was permanently beset with
great difficulties. Its proscription was the least of our worries. An
illegal print shop was fitted out, where the *Rote Fahne* was produced. But as the paper's proscription made normal distribution
impossible, it could only be sent in parcels, which even from Leipzig
only arrived in Berlin after three or four days or even later. If the
paper was sent by couriers they were all too frequently arrested
and the newspapers confiscated. The distribution too had to be carried
out illegally, as any newspaper vendor who sold copies of the *Rote
Fahne* was arrested. In addition there was the difficulty in getting
paper. Paper for printing purposes, like everything else at the time,
was rationed and only obtainable against coupons. The Reich supply
department obviously did not hand out paper for the illegal *Rote
Fahne*. This made us dependent on the black market which was
very expensive.

The decisive factor, in addition to all these hindrances, came
when the state of siege was extended to Saxony. The authorities
hesitated for a little while so as not to disturb the spring [Leipzig]
trade fair. Early on 11 May, while still half asleep, I heard the tramp
of horses. As I looked out of the window, Maercker's[8] troops were
patrolling in front of the *Leipziger Volkszeitung*, which was opposite my flat.

As all our meetings in Leipzig had been kept strictly confidential, and my flat which also served as office was known only
to a few reliable party comrades, it was only the official Communist Party office that was occupied by the Maercker soldiers, after
all the most important documents had been removed. But the print
works of the *Rote Fahne* was demolished.

As it happened, the leading political comrades had gone to Berlin
for discussions before the arrival of General Maercker. After waiting
several days, and once we had brought everything into order and
packed all the material, I also left for Berlin, together with the other
comrades who had remained in Leipzig. For security reasons I stayed
with friends. When I arrived at my illegal flat I heard that Rosa
Luxemburg's body had been found in the Landwehr canal. This
was also reported in the papers. Though there had already been
several such rumours, which on investigation proved to be false,
this time the news seemed true. Noske,[9] moreover, had the dead
body taken to Zossen; he must have had an interest in the lifeless
corpse. Did he plan to bury Rosa Luxemburg somewhere surrep-
titiously?

To find out more I went to Theodor Liebknecht's office. He
had himself gone to Stuttgart, where he had undertaken to appear

for Communist defendants in a political trial. The Garde-Kavallerie-(Schützen)-Division had already agreed to take a doctor of our choice by car with them to Zossen, to examine the post-mortem findings of the official physicians. Theodor Liebknecht's understudy declined this. To accept, he thought, granted the Garde-Kavallerie-(Schützen)-Division the right to present itself as a court of law. I did not share this opinion: the finding of the post mortem was important, possibly enabling conclusions to be drawn on the manner of assassination. I insisted therefore that a physician in whom we had confidence should be present at the post mortem of the official physicians.

In the meantime it had got late. I asked two doctors in vain to travel with the officers to Zossen. They feared for their lives; it was certain they would have to reckon with political persecution. One of the two doctors had agreed, but withdrew his promise with the excuse that he could not miss an important operation next morning. I tried my luck with a third doctor with whom we were on friendly terms, and he immediately declared his readiness. He assured me that he definitely did want to go. In addition I phoned the son of Clara Zetkin, Dr Maxim Zetkin,[10] at the Schöneberg hospital where he worked as a doctor. I wanted to ask him to accompany his colleague. But Dr Zetkin had left and there was no way of reaching him. The next day I learned that the doctor who had given me a firm promise had not after all gone to Zossen. The lawyer Dr Weinberg had dissuaded him, again with the reasoning that the Garde-Kavallerie-(Schützen)-Division should not be recognised as a court of law.

In the meantime the post mortem had taken place. I asked Maxim Zetkin to obtain permission from the Garde-Kavallerie-(Schützen)-Division to subsequently inspect the body on which the post mortem had been carried out. He went to the ill-famed quarters of the division, the Eden Hotel,[11] where he was first shown a few objects taken from the dead body about which he knew nothing. Having been mostly away from home, he had seen Rosa Luxemburg only occasionally at his mother's. He could not even identify Rosa Luxemburg from the pictures presented to him — the body had been photographed. He proposed to the officers he was discussing with that I should come.

I at once recognised the objects shown to me: a pair of gloves which I had bought, a scrap of a velvet dress which had not faded, and a gold clasp which had been taken from the body undamaged. I was also given some photos which I handed to Paul Levi without a glance at them. There was no doubt, he said on looking at the photos, that it was the body of Rosa Luxemburg.

I was given a paper which ordered the release with the words that the body was released by the military authorities; whether Herr Noske would release it was doubtful. Now it was a case of acting quickly. I contacted the lawyers with the request not to concern themselves any more with Rosa Luxemburg's body. It had been released, everything else I would do without their help. "I have already written to Noske," one of the lawyers remarked, "he should release the body to you. Why not await his decision?" It was precisely this decision that I did not want to await. Fearing they might not hand over the body in Zossen, I asked Paul Levi whether I should take a hearse. Paul Levi wanted me to make the attempt immediately. It was now too late for that day, I could only start the sad journey the next morning, with Maxim Zetkin accompanying me. At the right place we showed the paper issued by the military authorities for the release of the body. Maxim Zetkin was allowed to see the corpse, but he could not establish anything further. The morgue attendant likewise could not carry out his duty, so far had the decomposition advanced. The body was covered with a cloth and a pillow placed below the head. Had the dead Rosa Luxemburg lain in the water all this time? What misdeeds had been committed on her?

It was only ten years after this dreadful discovery, in the case of the state attorney Jorns,[12] that Paul Levi could explain the facts in full detail. This trial was initiated by Jorns, offended by the accusation of a journalist that he had favoured the murderers of Rosa Luxemburg and Karl Liebknecht. The case was conducted by Paul Levi, who by reviewing the files could establish the brutality with which the dehumanised officers had proceeded with the murder, in such a way that the public now learned how all these crimes had been covered up, the officers helped to acquittal or escape, and the guilt of the instigators and murderers hushed up; and how the leader of the court martial initiated after the murder, the then court-martial counsellor Jorns, remained in office and rose ever higher. Paul Levi was unable to continue this case to its end. *
He met his death in tragic circumstances, not far from the place where the dehumanised rabble of soldiers had thrown the brutally murdered Rosa Luxemburg into the water.[13]

Maxim Zetkin returned from Zossen to his place of work whilst I travelled to the morgue in Berlin, sitting next to the driver. The

* *Der Jorns-Prozess. Rede des Verteidigers Dr Paul Levi nebst Einleitung,* Berlin 1929, Internationale Verlagsanstalt.

route went through Lichtenrade, resplendent in its spring colours, past woods and meadows where Rosa Luxemburg had spent happy hours. The hearse also went through Südende and past the *Rote Fahne* building in Berlin, Rosa Luxemburg's last place of work. <A few doors away from this I asked to stop in front of a garden shop where I had often bought flowers to put on Rosa Luxemburg's desk. Now I bought a bunch of white lilac and had it placed on the coffin.> Then we handed over the coffin to the morgue, where I went daily to check that the body was still in its place.

The day of the burial arrived. Workers carried the coffin on an open carriage covered with wreaths. I followed a short stretch on foot and then went to Clara Zetkin. She had come to say the last words of farewell to her friend at the grave. <She did not take part in the powerful march which moved on from Friedrichshain. Her car passsed through the streets in front of the march, where a solid mass of proletarians were waiting on the pavement, and, prevented from joining the procession, said a last farewell to their leader.>

The enormous funeral march which set out from Friedrichshain became a powerful demonstration of the revolutionary workers. At the head were sailors and soldiers in battle grey, then followed the closest friends and party comrades, joined by the Berlin districts and factories. In front of the cemetery the funeral march dissolved. Only a restricted number of cards had been issued for the interment. Paul Levi spoke first at the open grave of the dead fighter and friend. Clara Zetkin followed him. A former student of the [SPD] party school remembered the beloved and honoured teacher. The youth representative included in her speech the hymn of Heinrich Heine:[14]

I am the sword, I am the flame.
I lit up the darkness for you, and when the battle began
I fought in the front rank.
All around me lay the bodies of my friends [...]
But we have time neither for joy nor for mourning.
The trumpets sound anew, a new struggle begins [...]

Then red flags were lowered on the grave of the dead heroine, to the sound of the *Internationale*.

Paul Levi, c. 1914

7. Memorial Speech by Paul Levi

Introductory note by Mathilde Jacob:

> It is no accident that in the awakening consciousness of
> nations, it is not battlefields, kings or marshals that have
> lasting significance; like ivy, the memory of nations winds
> itself round grey prison walls and the simple human
> martyrdom they contain: the Tower of London, the Bastille,
> the Spielberg and now the Schlüsselburg

— Paul Levi on Vera Figner's *Nacht über Russland*[1]

On 2 February 1919, in the Teachers' Union building in Berlin,
Paul Levi delivered the memorial address for Rosa Luxemburg and
Karl Liebknecht.[*] In the words that follow he gave a presentation
of the life and achievement of these two great departed that will
be valid for all time.

In the decisive years of his life Paul Levi stood in close connection with Rosa Luxemburg in her political work. Shortly before his demise he had the opportunity to present once more the
bloody drama of the German revolution in which so many courageous people found a martyr's death along with Rosa Luxemburg
and Karl Liebknecht. In his speech at that trial, which can be described as classical, he was able to expose the brutal murder of
Luxemburg and Liebknecht in all its details.[2]

The biographical part of Paul Levi's memorial speech — Leo
Jogiches gave his friend and comrade-in-arms the information on
the personal life of Rosa Luxemburg — is given in these pages as
an appendix to the present book, which is intended only as testimony of a love for Rosa Luxemburg as a person beyond the grave
as well as for a cause of which we must say, remembering all the
victims, that the revolution and civil war brought us much pain,

[*] Paul Levi, *Karl Liebknecht und Rosa Luxemburg zum Gedächtnis.*
Rede, gehalten von Paul Levi bei der Trauerfeier am 2. Februar 1919 im
Lehrer-Vereinshaus zu Berlin. Hrsg. Von der Kommunistischen Partei
Deutschlands (Spartakusbund) [Berlin 1919].

and — we may say for our part — disappointment with our class comrades.

* * *

Paul Levi:

Rosa Luxemburg was born on 5 March 1871,[3] the daughter of a Jewish merchant of Zamosc, in Russian Poland. Her parents lived in impoverished circumstances. In her youth she learned the meaning of poverty. Yet this was poverty of a rare kind! For despite this poverty her family raised itself noticeably above the level of its surroundings. This was not the obscure and timid milieu in which the Jewish community customarily lived there in Poland, in this lowly house was an environment of genuine intellectual life. It may have been from her mother's side that a spirit of intellectualism prevailed. In this household, despite its poverty, earthly goods were viewed with indifference; rather than counting money, it was the mind that was cultivated; they spoke Polish, not Yiddish, and instead of reading the Talmud, they read the German classics, Schiller and Goethe, as well as Polish literature.

It was a poor household, yet it displayed a rare close and faithful family life; the connections with the mother seem to have been especially warm. We know with what tenderness Rosa wrote and spoke of her mother. The parents sought to obtain the best education for their children that was possible in Russia. In this way Rosa came to attend the Grammar School for Girls in Warsaw. There she showed in her earliest years the characteristic that was later to astound anyone who came into contact with her: an acuteness of understanding that was without parallel. In all classes at the school she was the youngest and smallest, yet she always took first place and received commendations through to the final class. They wanted to award her the gold medal for her achievements, but this was ruled out as politically she was not as inconspicuous as was required in Russia — that was her first political sacrifice. Politics, which was the passion of the then awakening generation in Poland and Russia, had gripped her early on. True, when she left the Grammar School at fifteen, she seemed inclined in other directions. She had a developed talent for drawing and occupied herself with creative writing. But as well as this more playful activity, she also joined one of the political 'circles' that flourished in Russia and Poland at the time. It was not yet socialist writers that they read there, but the writings of liberal politicians. Even that, however, was enough for the Russian police. Her circle was dissolved by police intervention, and at the age of eighteen Rosa Luxemburg had to flee across the frontier, making for Zurich, a city that was then still a place of asylum for political refugees of all lands. There she began an irregular university study, focusing first on mathematics and natural sciences, for which she had already shown a particular inclination and talent as a school student.

In Zurich she found for the first time a path to the great ideas of socialism. In part it may have been the contact with Polish and Russian friends that showed her the way, but it was also and above all contact with a family on which I believe I must say a few words. The Lübecks were poor German Social-Democrats, who had likewise reached Zurich as refugees and had there been pursued by hard personal misfortune. The husband was a complete invalid and lay disabled in bed; he was no longer able to write. The wife was prey to internal conflicts and alienated from family life; the family presented a picture of dissolution and destruction. There were also a flock of children. Rosa Luxemburg entered this household first of all as a lodger. From home she had only the most modest means, and could not help the Lübecks materially. But the most characteristic aspect of her nature already showed itself here: from the moment of her entry into this household she became the family's moral support; she, the little one, was the strongest, the strong soul to whom others could turn. She helped the severely ill husband, who was unable to write, by writing for him or at his dictation, she supported the wife in her conflicts and kept her within the family, she gathered the children round her, built up what had decayed and held the family together again. She did already at that time in that small circle what she later did in large political parties: her strength of character raised up all wandering and wavering spirits to new, steady and firm life.

In this household and in contact with Herr Lübeck she also found the further way that led her towards socialism. No one transmitted this to her: she gleaned it from the sources, from the works of Marx and Engels themselves, which she read in these years.

Without systematic university studies, she spent the following years, from 1889 to 1892, partly in Zurich, partly in Bern, partly in Geneva, basically occupied with studies of socialist and historical literature. In those years she also came into contact with Russian socialists, in particular with Axelrod[4] and Plekhanov.[5] In 1892 she returned again to Zurich, and this year brought her entry into political life. She joined a small circle of Polish socialists, Karski [Julian

Marchlewski], Leo Jogiches and other friends, who remained faithful to her to the last day of her life, and undertook together with them to influence the Polish movement and introduce the work of Karl Marx into the political life of Poland.

Until this time there had not been in Poland a specifically Marxist tendency. Those groups that called themselves socialist were small terroristic and conspiratorial groups; nowhere was there a party based on the movement and the actual life of the masses. The prevailing tendency was that led by Dazynski,[6] which believed that the way to social revolution in Poland lay via the detour of the establishment of an independent Polish state.

This is where her work began. In her circle she was right away the intellectual leader, and took on the task of writing a pamphlet for May Day of 1892.

Such May Day pamphlets had a particular significance. In what was then the Russian empire the stoppage of work and demonstration on 1 May was the only opportunity for socialist parties to show their strength and develop. It was a yardstick of the strength of the movement, similar to how in Germany the Reichstag elections served as such a measure. Because of this importance, May Day was always greeted with a particular literary work, and for 1892 it was Rosa Luxemburg who produced this work. It was her first political-literary work and at the same time the only one that could not be printed — when she delivered the manuscript, it turned out that instead of being in prose, it was written in hexameters.[7]

Rosa Luxemburg now began a struggle against a world of enemies. In 1893 appeared the first Polish socialist paper, *Czrawa Robotnitscha* (Workers' Cause).[8]

Its publication signalled the beginning of the struggles within Polish Social-Democracy. The leading force in Poland at that time was the above-mentioned party of Dazynski, which had as its immediate aim the establishment of a Polish national state and considered this Polish state as the precondition for the liberation of the proletariat. It attacked most bitterly the newly emerging Marxist tendency; and initially with success.

In 1893 Rosa Luxemburg was sent as a delegate to the International Socialist Congress in Zurich, and experienced the charade of being excluded from the congress by the secretariat at the instigation of Dazynski, supported moreover by the German delegation, on the grounds that hers was a police organisation. She did not let this scare her off. The struggle for Marxism in Poland had to be waged from the bottom up. Rosa Luxemburg wrote the theoretical and historical works. In profound studies of Polish history she laid the theoretical basis for a Marxist movement in Poland. By indicating the entire historical background of Polish development, including the social background of the Polish rebellions and all the economic developmental tendencies of the present time, she raised the question whether the re-establishment of a Polish state was possible, and whether the proletariat had the task of founding national states, or should it not in Poland fight against absolutism in closest connection with the Russian proletariat, as well as together against the bourgeoisie. She worked at this time — 1895 — in Paris, studied there the sources on Polish history in the Bibliothèque Nationale, and her works found their conclusion in two texts of which one, 'The Industrial Development of Poland',[9] is of fundamental theoretical importance, while the other practical-agitational text forms the conclusion of her years of Polish journalistic activity: 'Social Patriotism in Poland' published as a series of articles in the Neue Zeit.[10] Here she developed the Marxist programme for Poland.

This was no small struggle, though from outside appearance it seemed to be waged just by Rosa Luxemburg. For Dazynski did not stand alone. Kautsky stood on his side. The German party leadership — at that time the world power in the International — supported him and opposed Rosa Luxemburg. Yet she had her success. In three years, by 1896, the work of founding Marxist socialism in Poland was accomplished. In that year she already experienced in London the triumph of her mandate being recognised at the congress of the International, in 1896–97 the German party leadership was won over, and in 1900 she experienced in Paris the further triumph of the new tendency being recognised on an equal basis with the old, as a group with the same rights as the Dazynski group. It was however in 1905 under the blows of revolution that the new orientation found its historical justification; the patriotic, nationalist tendency in Polish Social-Democracy was condemned in the revolution to insignificance. Under the blows of the revolution and those of the agitator Rosa Luxemburg, Polish social-patriotism split and subsequently remained insignificant until the 'liberating work' of Bethmann-Hollweg and Beseler brought it a certain new blossoming, which faded all the more quickly.[11] Rosa Luxemburg always remained true to the Polish movement. Until 1912 she helped her Polish friends with regular literary work, and still later, even from prison. Certainly, in Poland as everywhere, the nationalist jackals ventured into light again during the war. But the coming revolution in Poland will be victorious against the patriots there too, it will march on and conquer under the banner that Rosa Luxemburg gave Polish Social-Democracy.

When in 1896 she had achieved the most difficult part of the struggle for Marxism in Poland, and had completed the theoretical basis, she turned the greater part of her energy to new tasks. The better to support the Polish movement, she intended to enter the German party, and so decided to move to Germany. The opinion in her circle in Zurich at that time was that if one wanted to be taken seriously in the German Social-Democratic Party, it was necessary to have a doctoral degree. In 1896 Rosa Luxemburg thus began to attend the Zurich university on a regular basis, and on 1 May 1897 she graduated 'magna cum laude' as doctor of law. Her professor indeed awarded her 'summa cum laude', but the faculty heads decided that this was too much for a woman. This gave her one pillar for her existence in Germany. Another was still needed, however. It was impossible to be active as a Social-Democrat in Germany as a foreigner, she would have to obtain German nationality. Nothing was easier than this. In the Lübeck family, as mentioned above, there was a whole host of sons, and with one of these young Lübecks Rosa Luxemburg underwent a marriage of convenience.[12] In this way she gained German nationality. The following day Rosa Luxemburg travelled to Germany, and the marriage was dissolved immediately after.

In 1898 Germany faced elections to the Reichstag. Rosa Luxemburg immediately engaged in the election campaign; her first activity was agitational. In Upper Silesia she was able to apply herself right away in the service of the Polish proletariat. Then however began her decisive activity in the party. The elections were over, and at one stroke she found herself immediately in the field in which she was strongest, theoretical polemics. It was in this year of 1898 that Eduard Bernstein published for the first time his essays *Problems of Socialism*, the theoretical basis of revisionism.[13] The strong edifice of the German party, which then seemed so powerful and solid, started to vacillate violently. Kautsky, then the theorist of note, became uncertain, the party leadership wavered. Here Rosa Luxemburg was on the large scale what she already had been in the small drama of the Lübeck family: the support of all waverers and weaklings. She published in the *Leipziger Volkszeitung* a series of articles, 'Social Reform or Revolution?'[14] These articles made their mark. They had a double success. They held the leading bodies of the German party firmly to the revolutionary line, and they made their author into the acknowledged leader of a tendency. For the time being, she took the wind out of the sails of revisionism in the party.

The two editors of the *Dresdener Volkszeitung* were deported from Germany at this time, and Rosa Luxemburg took over as their successor.[15] Yet she remained only a short while in this position and then settled in Berlin as a free writer. Here she was able once more to repeat the polemic against Bernstein in a more fundamental form, when he published his book.

In the meantime, however, a second danger threatened socialism. In 1900 Millerand[16] entered the French government of Waldeck-Rousseau,[17] which raised the question of ministerialism in the International. Jaurès,[18] the strongest leader of French social-democracy, defended ministerialism, he was for the entry of socialists into bourgeois governments, and thus gave new strength in all countries to the opportunism that had just been defeated. [August] Vollmar[19] likewise defended this in the *Sozialistische Monathefte*. No opponent was to be found in Germany, so Rosa Luxemburg entered the field. She waged this struggle in five articles in the *Neue Zeit*.[20] With a dismissive gesture she pushed Vollmar aside and sought out the real and strongest opponent in this struggle, Jean Jaurès. Her success was such that in 1904 at the International Congress in Amsterdam the question of ministerialism was decided in the revolutionary sense and all life that opportunism of all countries had drawn from ministerialism once again disappeared. Jaurès was defeated and had to accept this.

1905 brought the Russian revolution. It began with the memorable procession of Petersburg workers under the leadership of Father Gapon outside the imperial palace.[21] Liberal demands were raised, for a representative assembly, freedom of press and assembly and the like. In a series of articles in *Neue Zeit*, Rosa Luxemburg raised the question, what is the task and the aim of the proletariat in the revolution, and she answered the question in the way that it has subsequently been answered both in Russia and in revolutionary circles throughout the world: the participation of the proletariat in the revolution has the aim of the dictatorship of the proletariat.[22] With this work she created not just the theoretical skeleton for the proletarian revolution in Russia, which began in October 1905, but also gave the theoretical goal for the revolutionary movement in which we stand at this moment and through which the proletariat of the whole world will have to pass in this year.[23]

But Rosa Luxemburg was not content with a theoretical leadership. Despite the warnings and advice of her friends, she travelled to Warsaw in December 1905 as Frau Matschke, took part in the movement there and was arrested in March 1906. She remained in prison until the end of June that year, when she was freed on bail. The fate that threatened her was clear: Leo Jogiches, her companion in this struggle, was condemned by the Russian courts at that time to the highest penalty of eight years in the penitentiary; the same would have been Rosa Luxemburg's fate. She made her way to Finland and from there via Sweden to Germany.

She now needed to summarise the lessons that the Russian revolution had given her and the German proletariat. This she did in a comprehensive literary activity. The first fruit was the pamphlet published in Hamburg, *The General Strike and German Social-Democracy*.[24] From the Russian revolution Rosa Luxemburg brought the new tactic through which alone the proletariat could complete its liberation struggle: the tactic of the mass movement, of mass action, of the mass strike in particular. From the day that she proclaimed this tactic, her relationship to the 'leading bodies' became a tense one. For the attitude of the German party leadership was expressed by Auer:[25] 'General strike; general nonsense.' The leadership felt that something new and bigger than party secretariats was being born, and they feared this new creation. They felt that with the entry of the masses into the movement a new element of unbridled force would arise, and feared these impetuous masses in their instinctive desire would shatter the artificial edifice constructed out of regulations and membership cards. Thus the struggle for mass action was at the same time a struggle against the party leadership. Despite this, however, for a time she prevailed on the party theoretically. Karl Kautsky turned towards her and wrote *The Way to Power*,[26] the only one of his books that others still read today and that *he* has completely forgotten. She continued the struggle at the party congresses. The year 1910 brought the crisis. There was the movement for general suffrage in Prussia, and for the first time in Germany the masses came onto the streets.[27] Herr von Jagow[28] decreed that 'the streets are only for traffic', the party leadership backed down, and all the energy of the masses dissolved into air.

From this Rosa Luxemburg drew the critical conclusions that she expressed in sharp criticism of the cowardly behaviour of the party leadership in a speech in Frankfurt of 1911; she repeated this criticism, in yet sharper form, in three articles in the *Dortmunder Zeitung*.[29] From this day on, her path diverged from that of the party leadership. Individuals parted company, and this was also a moment of decision for the theoretical light of the party, Karl Kautsky. Under the influence of the Russian revolution he had come close to Rosa Luxemburg's standpoint. Now he was also faced with the question: for revolution with the masses, or for the party leadership with membership cards? In his series of articles on 'Offensive or Attrition', he took his stand with the party leadership and thus set out on the path that would lead him *together* with the leadership towards 4 August 1914.

At this point I must put in a word on her activity at the party school founded by the SPD. She was the best teacher, she was the leading theoretical mind and temperament, and I believe there was scarcely a more pleasant memory in Rosa Luxemburg's life than in 1913 when Eduard Bernstein sought to have her dismissed from this post. Man for man (these were grown-up students), whether they remained her supporters or subsequently turned against her, the students supported Rosa Luxemburg and gave such a testimony for her that even a German party leadership had to abandon the idea of dismissing her.

New struggles now began. The times had changed. Half measures and empty words were no longer tolerable. On the distant horizon appeared the first clouds of the storm that would explode in this war. Imperialism had generally become *the* question of socialist politics. Rosa Luxemburg was one of the first to consider this question, already in 1905, and recognised its full significance. In the years after 1910 she entered into direct struggle against the war that had to come. She struggled in theory and in practice. On the theoretical side, she dissected imperialism in her work on *The Accumulation of Capital*,[30] on the practical side in her struggle against militarism. The former activity drew upon her the attacks of all press lackeys of the party leadership, which did not want to see imperialism and its dangers because of the unavoidable consequences these would have on the party and its political leadership; the latter brought attack by Prussian public prosecutors. The former ended in vitriolic newspaper articles, the latter in prison sentences. In autumn 1913 she again gave a speech in Frankfurt-am-Main in which she pointed out to the proletarians the dangers that faced them, and in which she spoke the words: "If we are expected to fire on our French brothers, then we say: No, we will not do this!"[31] This was a crime that was punished by the Frankfurt courts with one year in prison. She was not intimidated. Directly after this verdict new speeches: speeches against the dramas of German militarism which were played out every day in the barracks.[32] The public prosecutor responded with a new attack, he wanted to add a further penalty to the year in prison already imposed. The trial took place in Berlin, where the public prosecutor and the whole world would hear the voices of thousands whom militarism had already tormented in peacetime. But this was interrupted before long, and the public prosecutor's activity, which was so fruitful politically, came to a premature end. The war began, and the moment came that would unite Rosa Luxemburg in arms with the second whom we mourn today, and who met his death together with her, Karl Liebknecht. [...]

★   ★   ★

After praising the personality and political activity of Karl Liebknecht, Paul Levi closed his speech as follows:

The revolution proceeds along its road, a road marked out with milestones, and these milestones are hills of corpses.

The bourgeoisie could not but commit the crime; it has led the world into this torment, this chaos, this anarchy. We shall march out upright, with waving banners, when the criminals lie power-less on the ground. We shall march out with proud steps, for we know that the salvation and the future of humanity rests in the victory of our banners.

And in this hour of victory we shall have once again to look back on all those who have lived for us and have died for us. In-deed, they all died with that hour in mind. I know that both Rosa Luxemburg and Karl Liebknecht loved the knight Ulrich von Hutten, the man who championed the start of the new age with his strong blows and his sharp words. Just as he, shortly before he died, called his comrades-in-arms, so would these two dead, if they could still speak to us, give our souls strength and courage for new battles.

Clara Zetkin with Rosa Luxemburg, 1911

Appendix: Two Letters from Mathilde Jacob

The SED party archives from the former German Democratic Republic contain a substantial correspondence between Mathilde Jacob and other leading Spartacists, especially Clara Zetkin who lived in Stuttgart.[1] On 18 January 1919, when Clara learned of Rosa Luxemburg's death, she wrote a long letter to Mathilde that is published in the standard edition of her selected works.[2] Mathilde's response is especially significant in the expression of her feelings towards Karl Liebknecht, which go far beyond what she later wrote in her memoir.[3] It is clear that she blames Liebknecht's adventurism for the ensuing tragedy, and she indicates the depth of the divide that there was in the Communist Party at this early date, which would lead two years later to the departure of those who remained true to the 'Luxemburgist' tradition.

Under the prevailing repression, living political figures in this correspondence are generally referred to by pseudonyms, often with a change of gender. Thus Leo Jogiches is 'Frau Dr Müller', Paul Levi is 'Paula', Clara herself is 'Frau Dichter'. To aid comprehension the correct names have been reinstated here.

*　*　*

1) Mathilde Jacob to Clara Zetkin[4]

Berlin, 25 January 1919

My dear, dear, very honoured friend,
I was released today from my short accidental confinement. Though I have my old mother at home, my one thought when I was released from prison was: you can no longer hasten to Rosa, life has ceased to have a content for you. For the last five years I was accustomed to seeing everything beautiful that I saw for Rosa, and describing it for her. Every glance, every word, every letter from Rosa gave me a boost to life and action. Even in my prison cell I lived completely in the thought of Rosa, I was able for the

first time to properly appreciate her martyrdom over the
many years, and learned the dreadful news quite acciden-
tally like a bolt from the blue. Only in the last two days
have I read the papers again, so that I am not even properly
oriented. But one way or another, the frightful business is
fact, and the loss is indescribably great for us all.

Rosa was indeed for all of us the giving party. And just
like you, I am torturing my mind with self-reproaches. Just
in the last four weeks a Fräulein [Medi] Urban came to stay
with Rosa, in fact a friend of Hans [Diefenbach], to whom
Rosa extended love and friendship. The young girl had "my
room" in Südende and enjoyed the good fortune of being
able to live at Rosa's place freely and independently. There
would still have been room for me, and Rosa asked me
several times in vain to come to her. How I have to pay for
this now! But my nerves were so overwrought that I
thought I would spend the nights crying, and anyway I was
working each day from nine in the morning to midnight,
sometimes indeed even later. When Rosa was away from
home, I was of course again available to help her with a few
personal conveniences. On Sunday evening I spoke with her
alone by chance for a brief half-hour, and I had to tell her
how I suffered from all my stupidities. Rosa laughed her
silver-bright laugh and said it was good to let everything
out, she herself had all kinds of things on her heart after
Hans's death. Then I took a specially tender leave of her.
On Monday morning by accident I was illegally arrested in
the pogrom atmosphere, and I did not see Rosa again. Since
that time I've hardly eaten, and my head is so bare and
empty that even now it can scarcely comprehend that Rosa
is no longer in the world. Moreover the repulsive manner of
her death and the whole atrocity committed on the beloved
body is so fearful that suddenly I can no longer grasp it. I
only know that every nerve in me cries out for revenge, and
though I know that history itself will take revenge for the
crime of Ebert and Scheidemann, I am only too aware that
this revenge will step over the corpses of our best people.

Leo [Jogiches] already came to see me. I went through
your dear letter of the 18th with him. He will respond to all
your questions in detail. The poor man is so distraught, and
my poor head so stupid, that I'm setting pen to paper only
as much as I absolutely have to, just to write to you.

Tomorrow — Saturday — is the burial of the victims.

For Rosa there is an empty coffin next to Karl. All this I
learned only from Leo. The two of us will go together
tomorrow. We are good friends, and I have sworn to myself
to earn this friendship afresh each day. Now that I can do
no more for Rosa, I also want to try and find a place for
myself in the organisation. The road of politics is full of
thorns, and the people whom I have to work with often
repulse me. I always tell myself then that people are like
this because conditions have made them so, and hence it is
a sacred duty to improve these conditions.

   We are hopeful that Rosa's literary remains can be
published. Apparently the troops did indeed rummage
around in Rosa's flat. Hopefully however we can save the
papers, Kurt [Rosenfeld] will likely see to this,* and I won't
need to engage all my strength on this matter. Please, you
too collect all that you have, essays from the L.V. [Leipziger
Volkszeitung] etc., etc. I believe I have almost all the
articles from the [Social-demokratisches] Korrespondenz
that Rosa, Karski and Mehring published shortly before the
war. Then I will try and describe Rosa's imprisonment from
Barnimstrasse through to her release from Breslau, together
with the letters from this period or a portion of these. Leo
will try and get Paul [Levi] to write Rosa's biography.
Mehring would have been the person for this, but merciless
death will rob us of him in the next few days.[5]

   To earn money that she can no longer use, Rosa translated Korolenko's History of My Contemporary. She also
supplied an introduction to this, which will at least ensure
her the admiration of all cultivated people. The introduction is true Rosa. I will get the Paul Cassirer publishing
house to send you a copy tomorrow.

   Then Rosa had her Antikritik ready, though during the
war it did not find a publisher. She intended to publish a
second part of the Junius pamphlet, she had the material for
this together in her mind. All her works in prison are still
in the box that I am still awaiting from Breslau. I hope that
this will arrive, and then I will of course take it under my
protection.

   I hope that we can do everything that we have in
mind. But we must live in the present moment, as we may
soon not be living any more. Spartacus has the role of the

---

* I mean, he will undertake just the formal legal steps.

Jews persecuted in the ritual murder stories. And the Berlin population live in a witches' cauldron, with Ebert and Scheidemann playing the role of Satan with unheard-of success. The devil is driven out with Beelzebub, but the hunt goes over our dead bodies.

Just as an aside: the house searches here involved unprecedented theft of the most arbitrary kind. They stole from my apartment too all the money I possess, so that unfortunately I will only be able to send you the money in a few days' time. Your parcel incidentally has not yet arrived.

Leo will discuss with C[ostia] whether you should come. He is loth to burden you with the sacrifice. We will write about this again.

I am of course very, very sorry for poor Sonia [Liebknecht]. I honestly am fond of her. But a long time back I ceased to value Karl any more, he should not stand alongside Rosa. No one stands beside Rosa except perhaps Leo, and he too gazes at Rosa in admiration without ever reaching her level, distraught that she is so irreplaceable.

My hatred for Karl [Liebknecht] is well-founded. It is an emotional thing with me, but despite my political immaturity my emotions have never betrayed me. Our best people hate him. All this you will immediately understand when we can speak in person, in as much as you are likely not in the picture.

I know that Rosa was still able to reply to you. Your cry of the 13th came too late for me to convey to her. We all acted neglectfully, none of us can escape the blame. And Leo was just not there. So fate ran its course.

Good night, dear and very honoured Frau Zetkin. I don't know what I have written, but I really wanted to write, it was a need for me. I thank you most heartily for your friendship. It is a great gift that you extend this to me. I reciprocate it fully and wholeheartedly. Intellectually I stand so far below you that unfortunately I can offer you nothing in this way.

Please, also press Costia's hand for me, though I do not know him. But our love for Rosa binds us all.

Yours most devotedly,
Mathilde Jacob.

*   *   *

In her letter of 18 January 1919, Clara Zetkin had especially asked Mathilde to do all that she could to safeguard Rosa Luxemburg's manuscripts. Mathilde succeeded in this task, and became indeed the legal custodian of Rosa's literary remains. This led to complications two years later, when Mathilde was expelled from the Communist Party as a supporter of its former leader Paul Levi, who had sought to hold the party to Rosa Luxemburg's principle of 'majority revolution' against the putschist tactics and authoritarian organisation imposed from Moscow. Clara Zetkin was sympathetic to Levi's position, and sought to mediate between Lenin and Levi when she visisted Russia in summer 1921.[6] But as positions rapidly hardened on both sides, Clara remained in the Communist Party, and her friendship with Mathilde, which had been especially close during the year Mathilde spent in Stuttgart,[7] declined to a cool formality.

In August 1921 the congress of the German Communist Party requested the leadership to undertake without delay publication of Rosa Luxemburg's works, but the leadership's response was that 'the practical execution of this will very likely be impeded by the fact that Rosa Luxemburg's literary remains are in the hands of a *fräulein* who no longer belongs to the party because of a breach of discipline. It is questionable whether she will supply us with the material.' This insult provoked Mathilde Jacob to a rare appearance in print, in a letter published in the Independent Social-Democratic Party's newspaper *Freiheit* on 5 September 1921, as printed below.

The breach became still more decisive a few months later, when with Mathilde's assistance, Paul Levi published Rosa Luxemburg's unfinished pamphlet on *The Russian Revolution*, with its resounding critique of Leninist policy. Ironically, while immediately after Rosa's death Clara had written to Mathilde that 'not a scrap of her papers must be lost,' she now attacked Levi for publishing this manuscript, on the grounds that Rosa had allegedly 'changed her mind' in the last weeks of her life.

*   *   *

2) Open letter in 'Die Freiheit', 5 September 1921[8]

[...] Many proletarians may well have asked themselves in some surprise who this *'fräulein'* might be who possessed Rosa Luxemburg's confidence to such a high degree that she was even appointed the guardian of her political papers. It goes against the grain for me to speak of myself. But I have always taken it for granted that one shoulders one's responsibilities and goes on doing so.

I marched as a simple soldier in the Spartacus League, but I never lost courage for the fight, I never left the work in the lurch like so many heroes of the 'offensive strategy'[9] who sit in the Communist Party leadership today. For years before the war I worked with Karl Liebknecht, Rosa Luxemburg, Franz Mehring and many others. In the most difficult time during the war I worked as unpaid secretary for Leo Jogiches. For the Spartacus League had no financial means, and all of us who fought in it and worked for it sacrificed our last penny and our utmost strength. It was a far more stressful work than today. We didn't come together for a banquet! We were sent to prisons and penitentiaries. How hard it was to gather contributions for the *Spartakus-Briefe*! Who apart from Rosa Luxemburg wrote for this publication? All communications for it went through my hands, and apart from very modest contributions from other parties, the only person besides Rosa Luxemburg who wrote for it was — the 'opportunist' *Paul Levi*.[10] He wrote from the trenches, from the barracks. At that time we didn't even have cover addresses.

Today a great many people have paraded their revolutionary heart and speak of me as '*fräulein*'. But why am I this '*fräulein*' and no longer a comrade? Apparently because I have signed as responsible publisher for Paul Levi's periodical *Unser Weg*. Yes, I admit quite openly my allegiance to Levi's tendency, but I have the same right as other comrades to know the reasons for my expulsion. Now, despite expulsion and all else I am no worse a comrade, and indeed could teach many 'comrades' a lesson.

Truly, were it not so tragic, it would be a joke that the present leadership of the Communist Party of Germany presents itself as the spiritual heir of Rosa Luxemburg.

Notes

Introduction

1) *Was will der Spartakusbund?* In Rosa Luxemburg, *Gesammelte Werke*, vol.4, Berlin [East] 1983, pp.440-9.

2) See below, p.96.

3) A selection of Rosa Luxemburg's letters to Sonia Liebknecht was published in English as early as 1921, and is reproduced in *Rosa Luxemburg Speaks*, New York 1971, pp.332-9. A broader selection of her letters from prison is to be found in S. E. Bronner, ed., *The Letters of Rosa Luxemburg*, Boulder 1978. Also in English is Elzbieta Ettinger's edition of RL's letters to Leo Jogiches, *Comrade and Lover*, Boston 1979, though these date from an earlier period.

4) 18 Sept 1915. Original in Rosa Luxemburg, *Gesammelte Briefe*, vol. 5, Berlin [East] 1984, p.75.

5) Letter to Hans Diefenbach, 5 March 1917. *Gesammelte Briefe*, vol. 5, p.183.

6) The biographies of Rosa Luxemburg available in English are Paul Frölich, *Rosa Luxemburg*, London 19.. (first published 1940); J. P. Nettl, *Rosa Luxemburg* (two volumes), Oxford 1966, (abridged pbk) Oxford 1969; Elzbieta Ettinger, *Rosa Luxemburg: A Life*, Boston & London 1987. Frölich writes as a political follower, whose book is now itself an historical document. Nettl's remains the standard work, politically sympathetic and with a wealth of references. Ettinger writes both as a woman and a fellow-Pole, who particularly appreciates Rosa Luxemburg's human qualities. Most up-to-date but not yet translated is Annelies Laschitza, *Im Lebensrausch, trotz alledem, Rosa Luxemburg*, Berlin 1996, which benefits from new material discovered in the last decade.

7) The book by Heinz Knobloch is *Meine liebste Mathilde. Die beste Freundin der Rosa Luxemburg* (5th edn, Frankfurt 1997), but besides a very discursive style, the author has not fully benefited from recent historical research. Mathilde Jacob has been discussed by several authors in the historical journal *IWK* (*Internationale wissenschaftliche Korrespondenz zur Geschichte der deutschen Arbeiterbewegung*), especially Ottokar Luban, 'Die "innere Notwendigkeit, mithelfen zu dürfen". Zur Rolle Mathilde Jacobs als Assistentin der Spartakus-Führung und KPD-Zentrale' (*IWK* 29:4, Berlin 1993). See also David Fernbach, 'Memories of Spartacus: Mathilde Jacob and Wolfgang Fernbach', *History Workshop* 48, autumn 1999.

8) The 'Kingdom of Poland' was the tsarist designation for the part of Poland annexed by Russia. In adopting this name for their party (subsequently

Social-Democratic Party of the Kingdom of Poland and Lithuania), Rosa Luxemburg and Leo Jogiches stressed their rejection of Polish nationalism.
9) See note 3 above.
10) Mathilde Jacob's correspondence with Clara Zetkin, Franz Mehring and other leading Spartacists is discussed by Ottokar Luban, op. cit.
11) Under the state of siege, Mathilde was held under administrative decree, the Prussian ministry of state ruling that: 'Mathilde Jacob acts in the interest of the Communist Party... Her activity is directed at the forcible overthrow of the legitimate government and the establishment of the dictatorship of the proletariat.' Ottokar Luban, op. cit., p.463.
12) See David Fernbach, 'Rosa Luxemburg's Political Heir', *New Left Review* 238, Nov.-Dec. 1999.
13) See Sybille Quack and Rüdiger Zimmermann, "Vorbemerkung" to Mathilde Jacob, 'Von Rosa Luxemburg und ihren Freunden in Krieg und Revolution 1914–1919', *IWK* 4/88, p.436.
14) Ibid.
15) Heinz Knobloch, in *Meine liebste Mathilde*, reconstructs the details of the deportation of Mathilde Jacob and her sister Margarete (Gretchen) from official records, including such things as the inventory of possessions that she was required to fill in before deportation, and a farewell note that Gretchen wrote to their neighbours.
16) See below, p.114.
17) Sybille Quack and Rüdiger Zimmermann, op. cit., pp.438-9.

1. The Birth of a Friendship

1) After emigrating from Poland to Switzerland in 1893, Julian [originally Julius] Marchlewski (1866–1925) was together with Rosa Luxemburg and Leo Jogiches a co-founder of the Social-Democratic Party of the Kingdom of Poland. He moved to Germany in 1896, where he collaborated with numerous left Social-Democrat journals. A co-founder of what became the Spartacus League, he was active in it until his arrest in 1916. After the Russian revolution he was expelled to Russia, and held high office in the early years of the Bolshevik government, before dying of typhus.
2) See Introduction, p.15.
3) Hugo Haase (1863–1919), lawyer, co-president of the SPD (together with Friedrich Ebert, following the death of its historic leader August Bebel in 1913), member of the Reichstag. From April 1917 a leading figure in the Independent Social-Democrat Party (USPD), and in 1918 a member of the Council of People's Commisars. Died of natural causes. Georg Ledebour (1850–1947), journalist for the *Vorwärts* and other Social-Democrat papers, member of the Reichstag, from 1917 a leading figure in the Independent Social-Democrat Party (USPD).
4) Karl Liebknecht (1871–1919), son of the SPD's historic leader Wilhelm Liebknecht, lawyer and campaigner against militarism, member of the Prussian parliament and of the Reichstag until his expulsion in 1916. Co-founder of the Spartacus League, murdered together with Rosa Luxemburg on 15 January 1919. See Introduction, p.15.

5) Otto Rühle (1874–1943), teacher, editor of Social-Democrat papers, 1912–18 leading member of the 'Bremen group', subsequently German International Communists, joined the Communist Party in 1919.

6) An account of these lectures is given by Wilhelm Pieck, *Gesammelte Reden und Schrften*, vol.1, Berlin [East] 1959, pp.330-1.

7) In *Faust*, Part One.

8) Rosa Luxemburg had lost her appeal against conviction in Frankfurt for an anti-war speech made there in September 1913. Before the wartime illegal activity began, therefore, she was already preparing for a 12-month stay in prison.

9) Mid-January 1915. Rosa Luxemburg, *Gesammelte Briefe*, vol.5, p.36.

10) In 1911, on the strength of her regular salary from the SPD party school, Rosa Luxemburg had moved to a five-room apartment in the pleasant district of Südende, a few stops on the suburban train from the city centre but already near the edge of Berlin at that time. As is clear from her correspondence, and occasional references in the present text, she was very attached to her home here.

11) See Introduction, p.14.

12) Rosa Luxemburg, *Gesammelte Briefe*, vol.5, pp.52-54.

13) See Introduction, pp.15-6.

14) See pp.122-3 below.

15) Richard Fischer (1855–1926), writer and Reichstag member from 1893 to 1919, head of the publishing and printing company Paul Singer & Co., and of the Vorwärts publishers.

16) Karl Liebknecht, Rosa Luxemburg, Franz Mehring, Clara Zetkin, 'Erklärung', in *Berner Tagwacht*, no.254 of 30 October 1914. Rosa Luxemburg, *Gesammelte Werke*, vol.4, p.5.

17) This press release from Karl Liebknecht could not be published in the Social-Democratic daily press. The oppositional Social-Democratic papers only carried a brief announcement of Rosa Luxemburg's imprisonment. This press release was first published in Rosa Luxemburg et al, *Briefe an Mathilde Jacob (1913–1918)*, edited and introduced by Narihiko Ito, Tokyo 1972, p.9.

18) To transport prisoners, also called 'green Minnie'.

19) Rosa Luxemburg, *Gesammelte Briefe*, vol.5, pp. 47-8.

20) Schiller, *Maria Stuart*.

21) Before the war Gertrud Zlotko lived in Rosa Luxemburg's flat as her housekeeper; Rosa also encouraged her as an amateur painter. In the straitened circumstances of war and imprisonment, Rosa had to let Gertrud go, as Mathilde explains below.

22) Charlotte Beradt ed., *Rosa Luxemburg im Gefängis*, Frankfurt 1973, p.115.

23) See Introduction, p.16.

24) In a note here Mathilde Jacob gives a reference to an edition of Rosa Luxemburg's speech at her Frankfurt trial, published by the Communist Party in 1920.

25) As was Mathilde herself, until January 1919. See below, pp.101-2/

26) English translation in *Rosa Luxemburg Speaks*, pp.257-331.

27) Rosa Luxemburg, *Gesammelte Briefe*, vol.5, pp. 78-9.

28) Adolph Hoffmann (1858–1930), Social-Democrat publisher, member of the Prussian parliament, a leading figure in the SPD left wing and from 1917 in the USPD. From November 1918 to January 1919 a minister in the Prussian government.

2. Five Months of Freedom

1) Sonia Liebknecht (1884–1964), Karl's Russian-born second wife and an art historian, was generally known in Germany as Sophie. A selection of Rosa Luxemburg's letters to her from prison are translated in *Rosa Luxemburg Speaks*, pp.332-9.

2) Hans Diefenbach (1884–1917), a friend of the Zetkin family, recipient of sentimental letters from Rosa Luxemburg in prison, killed in action as an army doctor during the Great War. See below, pp.63-4.

3) Mathilde Jacob quotes here a poem of Eduard Mörike, 'Auf einer Wanderung', not translated.

4) See section 1, note 2.

5) The two guidelines most often quoted are those reproduced at the head of the leaflets cited on pp. 43 and 47 below. Full version in *Rosa Luxemburg Speaks*, pp.330-1.

6) See above, p.24.

7) This leaflet that Mathilde Jacob attributes to Rosa Luxemburg was in fact authored by Karl Liebknecht. Karl Liebknecht, *Gesammelte Reden und Schriften*, vol.8, Berlin [East] 1958–68, pp.613-6.

8) Theodor Liebknecht (1870–1948), ran a legal practice in Berlin together with his brother Karl. Though not a Spartacist, he was an active member of the USPD.

9) The complete text of this leaflet appears in E. Meyer (ed.), *Spartakus im Kriege*, Berlin 1927.

10) Unlike most of the Spartacus leaflets, this is known only from Mathilde Jacob's citation here, though a leaflet of October 1916 is somewhat similar.

11) In his collection *Spartakus im Kriege*, Ernst Meyer credits Julian Marchlewski with the authorship of this leaflet (pp. 232 and 157-9).

12) Philip Scheidemann (1865–1939), who became co-president of the SPD in 1917–18, was from the start of the war a trenchant militarist, his name coming to serve the radical left as representative of his type, the 'Scheidemänner'.

13) See section 7, note 12.

3. Return to Prison

1) Eduard Fuchs (1870–1940), Social-Democratic journalist, art collector and cultural historian, active in the Spartacus League and later the German Communist Party.

2) Ernst Meyer (1887–1930), editor at *Vorwärts*, co-founder of the Spartacus League, member of the Communist Party leadership until his expulsion as a 'rightist' in 1928.

3) The *Briefe* originated in fact from leaflets produced by Rosa Luxemburg's group for the SPD constituency organisation of Niederbarnim which they controlled, and at this point they were duplicated on Mathilde Jacob's machine. They were retitled after Rosa Luxemburg's article 'The Politics of the Social-Democratic Minority', January 1916, signed 'Spartakus' (*Gesammelte Werke*, vol.4, pp.171-80), and eventually the group officially adopted this name.

4) Vladimir Korolenko (1853–1921), Russian writer and Menshevik socialist. Rosa Luxemburg's translation appeared after her death in 1919. Her Introduction is translated in *Rosa Luxemburg Speaks*, pp.340-64.

5) Late September 1916. *Gesammelte Briefe*, vol.5, p.136.

6) While the *Kommandantur* was the military office for the local district, the *Oberkommando* was the higher military authority for Berlin and the surrounding region.

7) Now Poznán in Poland.

8) The complete text of this letter is in *Gesammelte Briefe*, vol.5, pp. 37-8.

9) This was Juliette Carton de Wiart, whose husband Henry Carton de Wiart was a socialist parliamentarian, and justice minister in Belgium from 1911 to 1918. From May to September 1915 she was imprisoned in Berlin.

10) This was in fact Dr Ernst Dossmann (1883–1963).

11) Paul Cassirer (1871–1926), writer, art dealer and publisher, commissioned Rosa Luxemburg's translation of Korolenko (note 4 above), and contributed financially to her support in prison. Tilla Durieux (the stage name of Ottilie Godefroy, 1880–1971), was a celebrated actress who worked with the Max Reinhardt company. In the Second World War she was active in the Yugoslav resistance movement. Her memoir *Eine Tür steht offen*, Berlin [East] 1965 deserves English translation.

12) Adam Mickiewicz (1798–1855), a patriotic Polish poet whom Rosa Luxemburg admired despite her opposition to Polish nationalism.

13) Luise Kautsky (1864–1943), the second wife of Karl Kautsky ('the pope of Marxism'), but estranged from him by the time that Rosa Luxemburg broke with her husband politically in 1910. A writer and translator, in the 1920s she published a selection of Rosa Luxemburg's letters to herself and Karl.

14) Now Wrocláw in Poland.

15) Rosa Luxemburg, *Gesammelte Briefe*, vol.5, pp.287-8.

16) Mathilde Wurm (1874–1934), writer and left Social-Democrat, a member of the Reichstag from 1920 to 1933. Marta Rosenbaum (1869/70–1940), Spartacist supporter, helped to finance *Die Internationale*.

17) *Gesammelte Briefe*, vol.5, p.393.

18) See section 2, note 26.

4. Working with Leo Jogiches

1) Here Mathilde Jacob seems to contradict what she said in the previous paragraph about the growth of the Spartacus League. It would seem that after strong growth in 1916, the League entered a difficult period following

the wave of prosecutions against its activists in winter 1917–18.

2) In summer 1917, the German side made approaches to the republican Russian government for an exchange of prisoners. It might thus have been possible for Rosa Luxemburg to be released, as a former citizen of Russian Poland, and Julian Marchlewski as still a Russian subject. The attempt was successful in Marchlewski's case, but not for Rosa Luxemburg.

3) I.e. the Social-Democratic Party of the Kingdom of Poland and Lithuania, which Rosa Luxemburg and Leo Jogiches still nominally headed.

4) According to an information sheet of the Association of Social-Democratic Constituency Associations for Berlin and surroundings, no. 16 of 15 July 1917, the Dutch-Scandinavian executive of the Inter-national Socialist Bureau then calling for a peace conference was also seeking the release of Rosa Luxemburg.

5) At the request of the Austrian Socialist leader Victor Adler, a series of prominent Socialists (Hjalmar Branting, Camille Huysmanns, Emile Vandervelde) intervened with the provisional government in Petrograd for the release of Otto Bauer. Bauer was returned to Austria in September.

6) It is most likely that Jogiches is confusing here the Serbian member of the International Socialist Bureau Pavle Pavlovic (1886–1971) and Trisa Kaclerovic (1879–1956). Both were elected to the Bureau at the Basle conference of 1912. While Pavlovic was not caught up in the war, Kaclerovic was captured by Austrian forces in the first half of 1917, and released after three or four months to take part in the Stockholm conference.

7) On 17 March the Petrogad soviet issued the celebrated manifesto 'To the Peoples of the Whole World', with the aim of putting an end to the war by common action for peace. It succeeded in having the provisional government take up the peace slogan. On 11 April the executive committee of the soviet also decided to call an international socialist peace conference in a neutral country, to coincide with other socialist peace initiatives. The Bolsheviks and the German radical left rejected this peace initiative and the formula 'peace without annexations or indemnities', and worked for a special conference of the Zimmerwald left.

8) See setion 2, note 12.

9) At the general meeting of the Social-Democratic Constituency Association for Teltow-Beeskow-Storkow-Charlottenburg (a group of Berlin districts), a resolution was adopted on 18 June 1917 supporting the International Socialist Conference in Stockhom. It was decided at the same time to choose three delegates, and Rosa Luxemburg, Franz Mehring and Käte Duncker were elected. In the event only Käte Duncker attended the conference on 5–12 September.

10) This refers to the peace initiative of the 'Dutch-Scandinavian Committee' of the International Socialist Bureau, which on 15 May 1917 issued invitations to a peace conference in Stockholm. The initiative foundered on the travel ban imposed on socialists from the Entente countries.

11) On 9 July 1917 Otto Rühle asked the Reich Chancellor whether he would consider releasing Rosa Luxemburg as a member of the International Socialist Bureau. The request was finally rejected on 11 October 1917. Rosa Luxemburg *Gesammelte Briefe*, vol.5, p.266.

12) A Petrograd newspaper which at this time supported the policy of the provisional government to continue the war.

13) This letter was first published in *Sozialistische Politik und Wirtschaft*, 2nd July 1924.

14) See below, p.85.

15) Bertha Thalheimer (1883–1959), like her brother August a left Social-Democrat in Stuttgart before 1914, and a leading Spartacist activist.

16) Scherl was one of the three largest newspaper publishers, owning among other papers the *Berliner Lokal-Anzeiger.* See below, p.94.

17) See David Fernbach, 'Memories of Spartacus: Mathilde Jacob and Wolfgang Fernbach', *History Workshop Journal* 48, autumn 1999.

5. Revolution and Tragedy

1) There was in fact only one Russian Soviet Republic at this point in time.

2) Adolf Gröber, a Reichstag deputy of the Catholic Centre party, became a minister in the short-lived government of Prince Max von Baden, formed in October 1918 after the general staff informed the Kaiser of Germany's impending defeat.

3) This refers to the conference of revolutionary shop stewards in Berlin, which on 2 November rejected by 21 votes to 19 setting a date for a revolutionary uprising. See Eberhard Kolb, *Die Arbeiterräte in der deutschen Innenpolitik 1918–1919*, Frankfurt 1978, p.62.

4) Ewald Vogtherr (1859–1923), merchant, Reichstag member, joined the USPD in 1917.

5) Levi refers to a report in the *Vossische Zeitung*'s evening edition of 4 November 1918. On that day the USPD and Spartacus League called a demonstration which was attended by many employees from Daimler and the railway works.

6) August Thalheimer, like his sister Bertha (section 4, note 15), was a prominent Spartacist based in Stuttgart. In the 1920s a leader of the Communist Party of Germany until his expulsion as a 'rightist'.

7) The *Arbeiterpolitik* was the organ of the Bremen left radicals, which appeared from 1916 to 1919. Under the editorship of Johann Knief this was one of the few legally published papers of the radical opposition.

8) Julian Borchardt (1868–1932), Social-Democratic editor, before the war a member of the Prussian parliament, belonged to the International Communists of Germany, a pro-Bolshevik group that fused with the Spartacists to form the Communist Party of Germany.

9) This leaflet, with the headline 'Let's Have True Democracy!' and the concluding slogan 'Gemany — A Republic!', appeared without publisher's address.

10) Paul Levi, 'Wie es anfing' [How It Began] in *Almanach nebst Kalendarium für die Leser des Sächsischen Volksblattes* [a supplement to this newspaper], Zwickau 1928, p.33.

11) Emilie Jacob (1849–1933).

12) As note 10.

13) This was indicated in particular by a large majority vote against participation in the forthcoming Constituent Assembly.

14) English translation in *Rosa Luxemburg Speaks*, pp.426-7.

15) This was Martha (Medi) Urban (1894–1963), later the wife of Karl Kautsky, junior.

16) Dr Alfred Bernstein (1858–1922), surgeon and obstetrician, Social-Democratic member of the Berlin council before the Great War, founder of the Berlin Arbeitersamariter. After 1918 a sympathiser of the Free Workers' Union of Germany. This address was Blücherstrasse 13.

17) See *The Family Chronicle of Eugen Fernbach*, Heretic Books, London 1999, pp.65-69.

18) Eugen Leviné (1883–1919). Of Russian extraction, participant in the Russian revolution of 1905, a leading figure in the Spartacus League. In April 1919 Leviné led the Munich soviet in its final phase, and was judicially murdered after its defeat. See Rosa Leviné-Meyer, *Leviné: Life of a Revolutionary*, London 1973.

19) This division had been formed out of loyal remnants of the imperial army, and was brought to Berlin to repress the revolutionary movement.

20) It was in fact twelve days until Mathilde's release on 25 January.

6. Aftermath

1) This was the headquarters of the Communist Party, a few minutes away from the *Rote Fahne* building.

2) This was 8 March, Mathilde's birthday and subsequently International Women's Day, a festival that Clara Zetkin had herself proposed shortly before the war, and was given its date to mark the women's demonstration in 1917 that started the 'February' revolution.

3) See section 2, note 8.

4) Kurt Rosenfeld (1877–1943), Rosa Luxemburg's lawyer; a teacher at the SPD party school, member of the USPD, after the Great War an SPD member of the Reichstag, and for a short time Prussian justice minister.

5) This report appeared in 1929. Cf. Fritz Winguth, 'Leo Jogiches zum zehnten Jahrestag seiner Ermordung', *Leipziger Volkszeitung*, 9 March 1929. Mathilde Jacob slightly edited the memoir of this former leader of the radical youth movement in Neukölln.

6) This policeman, whose biographical details are unknown, was also responsible for the murder of the trade-union leader Wilhelm Sült, and the revolutionary sailors' leader Heinrich Dorrenbach. See *Illustrierte Geschichte der deutschen Revolution*, Berlin 1929, pp 367-8.

7) Georg Wagner (1867–?), active as a Social-Democrat in Hanau, worked as a doctor for trade-union organisations. He joined the Communist Party, and led a local group of supporters of Paul Levi after his expulsion in 1921. Thought to have died in concentration camp.

8) Georg Maercker (1865–1924), army general and a leader of the Freikorps.

9) Gustav Noske (1868–1946), a Social-Democratic journalist and Reichstag deputy, served as defence minister from January 1919 to March 1920, and was associated more than any other politician with the bloody suppression of the post-war revolutionary movements.

10) Maxim Zetkin (1883–1965) was the elder son of Rosa Luxemburg's friend Clara Zetkin.

11) This is where Karl Liebknecht and Rosa Luxemburg were brought after their arrest, and beaten senseless before being taken out to be shot.
12) Paul Jorns (1871–1942), a military lawyer, was in charge of the investigation into the murders of Karl Liebknecht and Rosa Luxemburg. Prominent in the early years of the Nazi regime.
13) Paul Levi's defence of his client accused of libel in the Jorns case was a triumphant success. In January 1930, however, the prosecution initiated an appeal, and midway through the proceedings Levi collapsed with pneumonia. A few days later, suffering a delirious fever, he fell to his death from the window of his attic flat.
14) Heinrich Heine, 'Hymnus'.

7. Memorial Speech by Paul Levi

1) Paul Levi, 'Ein Erinnerungsbuch', in Sozialistische Politik und Wirtschaft, 30 December 1926.
2) See section 6, note 13.
3) Paul Levi's original wrongly gives the date as 5 May, which Mathilde Jacob corrected here.
4) Pavel B. Axelrod (1850–1928), one of the founders of the first Russian Marxist group, the League for the Emancipation of Labour; later a leader of the Mensheviks.
5) Georg Plekhanov (1856–1918), leading Russian Marxist writer, later supported the Mensheviks.
6) Ignazi Dazynski (1866–1936), from 1892 leader of the Polish Socialist Party of Galicia and Silesia (PPSD), i.e. of the part of Poland under Austrian occupation. A deputy in the Austro-Hungarian parliament, and in November 1918 prime minister in the provisional government of the Polish Republic.
7) Despite Paul Levi's reference to this political verse, presumably on Leo Jogiches's good authority, the manuscript in question has never been discovered.
8) Levi means here the socialist monthly Sprawa Rabotnicza, which appeared irregularly in Paris from 1893 to 1896.
9) Rosa Luxemburg, Gesammelte Werke, vol.1/1, Berlin [East] 1982, pp.113-216. This was Rosa Luxemburg's doctoral dissertation at Zurich University in 1898.
10) Gesammelte Werke, vol.1/1, pp. 37-51.
11) Theobald von Betthman-Hollweg (1856–1921) was German Chancellor from 1909 to 1917. The Prussian general Hans von Beseler (1850–1921) was Germany's military governor in Warsaw from 1915 to 1918.
12) Rosa Luxemburg's legal husband was Gustav Lübeck. Though the marriage was dissolved in 1903, she continued to use his name as an occasional incognito.
13) Eduard Bernstein (1850–1932) had been a close friend of Frederick Engels in his last years, and was a leading figure in German Social-Democracy. Despite representing opposite poles of opinion within the SPD, Bernstein remained staunchly anti-militarist, and during the Great War sided with the opposition USPD. He wrote a respectful tribute to Rosa Luxemburg after her death.

14) English translation as 'Reform or Revolution' in *Rosa Luxemburg Speaks*, pp.33-90.

15) The two editors were Rosa Luxemburg's Polish friend Julian Marchlewski, and the Russian Alexander Helphand (aka Parvus).

16) Alexandre Millerand (1859–1943), journalist and parliamentarian, became in 1899 the first socialist member of a bourgeois government. He was expelled from the French Socialist Party in 1905, and was president of the republic in 1920.

17) Pierre Waldeck-Rousseau (1846–1904) was a moderate republican, and in his period as prime minister put through legislation separating church and state.

18) Jean Jaurès (1859–1914), from 1885 a deputy of the radical left, founder of the newspaper *Humanité*, one of the most respected figures in international socialism. Murdered in Paris on 31 July 1914, a martyr to his anti-war stand.

19) Heinrich Georg von Vollmar (1850–1922), a leading German Social-Democrat and Reichstag member from 1890 to 1918, moved from the left to represent the party's right wing.

20) English translation as 'Socialist Crisis in France', *Rosa Luxemburg Speaks*, pp.91-106.

21) G. A. Gapon (1870–1906), Russian priest, in fact an agent of the tsarist secret police, leader of the St Petersburg workers' demonstration in January 1905 that sparked off the revolution.

22) This does not seem to be a correct interpretation of Rosa Luxemburg's articles on the Russian revolution of 1905. See for example J. P. Nettl, *Rosa Luxemburg* (pbk edn), pp.229-31.

23) Here Paul Levi casually expresses the exaggerated revolutionary optimism of 1919.

24) English translation as 'The Mass Strike, The Political Party and the Trade Unions', *Rosa Luxemburg Speaks*, pp.153-218.

25) Ignaz Auer (1846–1907), a saddler by trade, secretary of the SPD executive from 1874, for many years a Reichstag member.

26) Karl Kautsky, *The Road to Power*,

27) Though Germany did not have a parliamentary government, the Reichstag was elected by universal male suffrage from the unification of 1871. The nineteen German states, however, continued to have substantial powers over domestic affairs, and the parliament of Prussia, the largest and dominant state, was elected on a three-class basis that was radically anti-democratic. Reform of the Prussian parliament was thus a key democratic demand until 1918.

28) Traugott von Jagow (1865–1941), police president in Berlin.

29) The speech referred to here, 'Der preussische Wahlrechtskampf und seine Lehren', was in fact delivered in Frankfurt on 17 April 1910. Two of the articles are reproduced in *Gesammelte Werke*, vol.2, Berlin [East] 1981, pp.334-343, but not the third article, "Die Lehren des Wahlrechtskampfes" of 14 April 1910.

30) English translation, *The Accumulation of Capital*, London 1951.

31) The text of this speech has not survived, but see J. P. Nettl, op. cit., p.321.

32) This refers to Rosa Luxemburg's denunciation of the brutalisation of conscripts.

Appendix: Two Letters from Mathilde Jacob

1) This correspondence is reviewed by Ottokar Luban (see Introduction, note 7), from where the two letters translated here are taken.

2) Clara Zetkin, *Ausgewählte Schriften und Reden*, Berlin (East), 1953, vol.2, pp. 71-74.

3) Cf. above, p.102, and Introduction, p.15.

4) Ottokar Luban, op. cit., pp.452-5.

5) Franz Mehring was terminally ill at the outbreak of revolution, and died a few days after Rosa Luxemburg was killed.

6) See Clara Zetkin, *Conversations With Lenin*, London 1929.

7) See Introduction, pp.17-8.

8) Ottokar Luban, op. cit., p.469.

9) The so-called 'offensive strategy', as applied in the disastrous 'March action' of 1921, led to Paul Levi's break with the Comintern.

10) In this polemical letter, so uncustomary for her, Mathilde Jacob exaggerates a little here, as above in her reference to working for Rosa Luxemburg for 'years' before the war.

Index

Lightning Source UK Ltd.
Milton Keynes UK
UKHW01f1303260818
327821UK00001B/100/P

9 780853 159001